PRAISE FOR *THE LINE BECOMES A RIVER*

"Lays bare, in damning light, the casual brutality of the system, how unjust laws and private prisons and a militarized border have shattered families and mocked America's myths about itself." —*New York Times Book Review*

"[Cantú] proves to be an astounding writer with this memoir for the moment." —*Entertainment Weekly*

"Veers away from propaganda and stereotypes and into the wild deserts and mountains, and, especially, the hearts and minds of the people who traverse the increasingly militarized borderlands." —*Wall Street Journal*

"A must-read for anyone who thinks 'build a wall' is the answer to anything." —*Esquire*

"Humanity is the preoccupation of *The Line Becomes a River*—recognizing it, acknowledging it, salvaging it." —*Washington Post*

"[Cantú's] beautifully written account of a life between nations cuts through the politics surrounding "the wall" to probe what's really at stake." —*O, the Oprah Magazine*

"A book that whips across your face like a sandstorm, embedding bits of the desert into your skin that, like it or not, you'll carry forward." —*San Francisco Chronicle*

"The best book on immigration you will read this year . . . honest, gripping and wonderfully written." —*Mother Jones*

"Exquisitely nuanced . . . explains the conflicted journey of a border crosser with an impressive level of compassion, self-reflection, and conviction." —*NBC News*

"Sharply political and deeply personal." —*New York Magazine*

T0038762

"A refreshing counterpoint to the glut of narco-thrillers and action-movie fantasies about US agents taking out drug dealers . . . and . . . a valuable contribution to the literature on what has become an increasingly scalding issue." —*New York Review of Books*

"If you read one book on immigration this year, choose *The Line Becomes a River*." —*Denver Post*

"Spare, graceful, and full of the details that propel a good story . . . [Cantú's] life on the line has made him the kind of expert we need to hear from." —*Boston Globe*

"Cantú's confessions mimic the desert landscape he patrols: haunting but elegant, with glimmers of humor for reprieve . . . The achievement of this book is how deftly Cantú reels us in, cold and wet behind him." —*Texas Observer*

"Raw and timely ... A striking picture of the unsparing borderlands." —*Minneapolis Star-Tribune*

"An insistently humane book, or maybe just a human one. . . . It's an exploration of how the border feels, and what happens to the people who get caught in its gears." —*Bookforum*

"Beautiful, eloquent and timely . . . [Cantú's] your correspondent if you want the real story." —*Cleveland Plain Dealer*

"The wall that separates us is high and wide, but as Cantú's memoir shows us, there is still a way around it." —*Los Angeles Review of Books*

"A poetic and empathetic work whose message—the border is built on an imaginary line, but its impact on the people who cross it, or can't, is real—feels more urgent this year than ever." —*Salon*

"By coming to better understand Cantú's fixation with the border, readers of his book are brought into that suspension, prompted—if not outright required—to experience what it's like to exist in-between, knowing no amount of politics or prayer can give a hard question easy answers."
—*CNN*

"Every single person in this country—near borderlands or not—should read this book, and realize that immigration cannot be solved with a single policy." —*Chicago Review of Books*

"Full of insights into the migrant experience." —*Financial Times*

"An intense and captivating memoir of dreams, divisions, and death at the border." —*Christian Science Monitor*

"A powerful, harrowing view of the border—a no man's land where no one returns the same. Run, don't walk, to your bookstore." —*KQED*

"[Cantú's] compelling, tragic account may help to break down the wall for others, too." —*The Economist*

"This work may determine for future generations what building a wall does to magnify the heartache of plight and flight, of people moving between nation and nationality . . . without the agency to define it themselves."
—*LitHub*

"This beautiful and horrifying memoir should be required reading."
—*New York Journal of Books*

"Cantú interrogates one of the thorniest subjects in contemporary America and finds his mother's warning to be true: 'We learn violence by watching others, by seeing it enshrined in institutions.'" —*The Week*

"[Adds] new depths to one of the most controversial issues of our modern times: the Mexican border." —*POPSUGAR*

"Fresh, urgent . . . A devastating narrative of the very real human effects of depersonalized policy." —*Kirkus Reviews (starred)*

"Cantú's rich prose and deep empathy make this an indispensable look at one of America's most divisive issues." —*Publisher's Weekly (starred)*

"A personal, unguarded look at border life from the perspective of a migrant and agent, recommended for those wishing to gain a deeper understanding of current events." —*Library Journal*

"There is a line dividing what we know and do not know. Some see the world from one shore and some from the other. Cantú brings the two together to a spiritual whole. My gratitude for this work of the soul."
—Sandra Cisneros

"A beautiful, fiercely honest, and nevertheless deeply empathetic look at those who police the border and the migrants who risk—and lose—their lives crossing it. In a time of often ill-informed or downright deceitful political rhetoric, this book is an invaluable corrective."
—Phil Klay, author of *Redeployment*

"Francisco Cantu's story is a lyrical journey that helps bridge the jagged line that divides us from them. His empathy reminds us of our humanity—our immigrant history—at a critical time."
—Alfredo Corchado, journalist, author of *Midnight in Mexico*

"Cantú's story, and intelligent and humane perspective, should mortify anyone who ever thought building a wall might improve our lot. He advocates for clarity and compassion in place of xenophobia and uninformed rhetoric. His words are emotionally true and his literary sensibility uplifting." —Barry Lopez, author of *Arctic Dreams* and *Of Wolves and Men*

"This book tells the hard poetry of the desert heart. If you think you know about immigration and the border, you will see there is much to learn. And you will be moved by its unexpected music."
—Luis Alberto Urrea, author of *The Devil's Highway*

THE LINE
BECOMES
A RIVER

RIVERHEAD BOOKS | NEW YORK

THE LINE
BECOMES
A RIVER

RIVERHEAD BOOKS | NEW YORK

THE LINE

BECOMES

A RIVER

FRANCISCO CANTÚ

RIVERHEAD BOOKS
An imprint of Penguin Random House LLC
penguinrandomhouse.com

Some of the material in this book originally appeared, in different form, in *Edible Baja Arizona*,
Guernica, *Orion*, *Ploughshares*, *J Journal: New Writing on Justice*, and *South Loop Review*.

Portions of the Author's Note originally appeared as "Cages Are Cruel. The Desert Is, Too"
in the *New York Times* on July 1, 2018.

Grateful acknowledgment is made to Les Figues Press for permission to quote from
Antígona González by Sara Uribe and to Cristina Rivera Garza and her translator, Jen Hofer,
for providing preliminary excerpts from the forthcoming English translation of *Dolerse*.

The Library of Congress has catalogued the Riverhead hardcover edition as follows:

Names: Cantú, Francisco, author.
Title: The line becomes a river : dispatches from the border / Francisco Cantú.
Description: New York : Riverhead Books, 2018.
Identifiers: LCCN 2017014247 (print) | LCCN 2017042308 (ebook) |
ISBN 9780735217720 (ebook) | ISBN 9780735217713 (hardback)
Subjects: LCSH: Cantú, Francisco (Essayist) | Mexican-American Border Region—Emigration
and immigration. | "Illegal aliens"—Mexican-American Border Region. | Border security—
Social aspects—Mexican-American Border Region. | U.S. Border Patrol—Officials and
employees—Biography. | BISAC: BIOGRAPHY & AUTOBIOGRAPHY / Cultural Heritage. |
BIOGRAPHY & AUTOBIOGRAPHY / Personal Memoirs.
Classification: LCC JV6565 (ebook) | LCC JV6565 .C37 2018 (print) |
DDC 363.28/5092 [B]—dc23
LC record available at https://lccn.loc.gov/2017014247
p.   cm.

First Riverhead hardcover edition: February 2018
First Riverhead trade paperback edition: February 2019
Riverhead trade paperback ISBN: 9780735217737
International edition ISBN: 9780525536253

Printed in the United States of America
9   10

Book design by Gretchen Achilles

To my mother and grandfather,

for giving me life and a name;

and to all those who risk their souls

to traverse or patrol an unnatural divide

PROLOGUE

My mother and I drove east across the flatlands, along the vast floor of an ancient sea. We had come to West Texas to spend Thanksgiving in the national park where my mother worked as a ranger during the years when I formed my first childhood memories—images of wooded canyons and stone mountains rising up from the earth, the sound of wind whipping across low desert hills, the warmth of the sun beating down upon endless scrublands.

As we neared the Guadalupe Mountains we passed an expanse of salt flats and I asked my mother to stop the car. She pulled onto the shoulder and we walked out together across broken earth. We stood looking north toward the Guadalupes, towering remnants of a Permian reef once submerged beneath the inland waters of Pangaea. A cool November wind blew against our bodies like a slow current of water and I bent down to touch the ground, breaking off a piece of white crust and rubbing it between my fingers. I touched my tongue and looked up at my mother. It tastes like salt, I told her.

Inside the park, my mother and I waited at the visitor center while a uniformed woman stood at the reception desk with a pair of visitors, patiently explaining the park's camping fees and hiking options. When the visitors turned to walk away, the woman caught sight of us and a smile spread across her face. She hurried over from behind the desk and reached out to hug my mother before taking a step back to look at me. She stood for a moment in disbelief. Ay mijo, the last time I saw you, you were barely this tall. She held her hand down at her knees. Are you still in Arizona? she asked us. Mom is, I said, but I went away for college in Washington. Her eyes grew wide. The capital? I nodded. Qué impresionante. And what are you studying? International relations, I told her. He's studying the border, my mother added. We're staying in El Paso on our way back so he can visit Ciudad Juárez.

The woman shook her head. You better be careful, she said, Juárez is dangerous. She stared at me with her hands on her hips and then reached out to touch my shoulder. You know, I still remember babysitting you when you were a little chamaquito. She looked down at my shoes. All you wanted back then was to be a cowboy. You would wear those little cowboy boots and that little cowboy hat and run around with my boys in the backyard, chasing each other with those little plastic guns. My mother grinned. I remember it too, she said.

The next morning, my mother and I woke early to hike through a canyon that stretched upward into the wooded backside of the Guadalupes. As we walked, my mother became a guide again, pointing at the quivering yellow leaves of a bigtooth maple, reaching out to touch the smooth red bark of a madrone tree. She bent down and plucked the dried shell of a dragonfly larva from a blade of grass and slowly turned it in her dirt-smudged hands. She looked up the trail toward the slow-rolling waters of the stream and began to speak to me of the glistening arthropod, explaining how it would have sloughed its skin to flit upon the swirling winds of the canyon. She cradled its exoskeleton in her hands like a sacred object. Dragonflies migrate as birds do, she told me, beating their papery wings for days on end across rolling plains, across long mountain chains, across the open sea.

My mother left the trail and sat on a rock at the edge of the stream, removing her shoes and socks. She rolled her pants to the base of her knees and waded into the water, tensing her shoulders at its coolness. She invited me to join her, but I shook my head and sat alone in the dappled sunlight on the bank. My mother stepped over rocks and fallen branches, pointing at the way the water flowed over an exposed root, the way the sun shone brightly on a clump of green grass. She bent over and touched the surface of the water, rubbing her wet hands on her face. As I collected fallen maple leaves, my mother reached down and pulled a handful of pebbled limestone from the streambed. Come, she called to me with dripping hands. Touch the water.

That night, as we sat in a backcountry research station eating precooked turkey and instant stuffing, I asked my mother why she had joined the Park Service all those years ago. She stabbed her fork at a piece of stuffing. I joined because I wanted to be outdoors, she told me, because the wildlands were a place where I could understand myself. I hoped that as a park ranger I could awaken people's love for nature, that I could help foster their concern for the environment. She glanced up from her plate. I wanted to guard the landscape against ruin, she said, to protect the places I loved. I sat back in my chair. And how does it feel now, I asked, looking back on it? My mother set down her fork and ran her finger along the wood grain at the edge of the table. I don't know yet, she said.

The following day, my mother and I left the park and drove west. As we came into El Paso that evening, I gazed out at the lights spreading across the floor of the desert valley, trying to make out where the United States ended and Mexico began. At our motel, a bespectacled clerk made small talk with my mother as he checked us in. What brings you to El Paso? he asked. My mother smiled. My son is researching the border, she said. The border? The man looked at us over the top of his glasses. I'll tell you about the border. He pointed beyond the glass doors of the motel to a grassy hillside at the parking lot's edge. You see out there? Used to be I would watch that grass move every night. Wasn't long before I realized it wasn't wind moving the grass, it was wetbacks sneaking across the line. The man smirked. But the grass hardly moves anymore, if you know what I mean. You don't see wets in people's yards these days. My mother and I nodded awkwardly as the man chuckled, handing us the keys to our room.

The next morning we parked at the Santa Fe Street Bridge and walked south toward the border. We followed a steady stream of crossers through a caged walkway that stretched over the concrete channel where the barely flowing water of the Rio Grande separated El Paso from Ciudad Juárez. As we neared the other end of the bridge, I watched as a bleary-eyed man said goodbye to his wife and son. The boy stood crying next to a groaning turnstile as his mother and father held each other in a long embrace. On the other side of the revolving gate, my mother and I were waved past an inspection table by a Mexican customs agent dressed in black. My mother turned to me. They don't want to see our passports? she asked. I shrugged. I guess not.

We left the port of entry and made our way down Avenida Benito Juárez past throngs of taxi drivers and snack vendors. We walked by blaring speakers and brightly painted storefronts—past liquor stores and pawn shops, dental offices and discount pharmacies, past taquerías and casas de cambio and signs advertising seguros, ropa, botas. After several blocks my mother asked if we could find somewhere to sit. We crossed the street to Plaza Misión de Guadalupe, where she quickly slumped down onto a bench. I need to catch my breath, she said, my heart's racing. Are you all right? I asked. She took in a breath and looked all around her, placing a hand on her chest. I'm fine, just a little overwhelmed. I glanced up at the sun. Listen, I'm going to get you some water. I touched her shoulder and pointed at a market across the street.

Inside the shop I stood behind two women discussing politics in the checkout line. I'm glad it will be Calderón, one woman said to the other. We need a president who will be hard on crime, someone to take on the delincuentes and clean up the streets. The other woman shook her head vigorously as she paid the shopkeeper for a carton of cigarettes and package of pan dulce. No entiendes, she said to her friend. The problem doesn't come from the streets.

My mother drank thirstily from the bottle of water, sighing

deeply as I consulted a pocket map we had taken from the hotel. We're close to Mercado Juárez, I told her, we can sit there and get something to eat while you rest. She nodded and took her time looking up and down the street before lifting herself from the park bench. We walked slowly down the sidewalk past the brick dome of the Aduana Fronteriza and turned to make our way down Calle 16 de Septiembre. A block from the mercado we stood at an intersection choked with cars, waiting for the signal to turn green. Then, as we made our way across four lanes of traffic, my mother cried out and fell to her hands in the middle of the street. I turned in panic and kneeled down at her side with my arms around her shoulders. Are you okay? I asked. She breathed through her teeth and gestured down at her foot, twisted in a pothole. You've got to get up, I told her, we've got to get out of the street. I looked up at the signal, flashing its red hand. I tried to drag her to her feet, but she shouted and winced, breathing in short gasps. It's my ankle, she said, I can't move it.

I stood in the intersection as the light turned green, holding my hands out to the line of cars. I glanced toward the mercado and saw a man running from the sidewalk. In front of us, a woman stepped out of her car and came to kneel at my mother's side. Tranquila, she whispered, tranquila.

A man in a cowboy hat stepped down from his idling truck and turned to the cars behind him, motioning for them to stand by. The man who had run from the mercado touched me on the back. Te ayudo, he told me, qué pasó? My hands were shaking as I gestured at my mother. No puede caminar. The man stood on the other side of her and made a lifting motion with his hands outstretched. We bent down together and slung my mother's arms around our shoulders. The woman at my mother's side reached out to touch her—vas a estar bien, she told her before turning to walk back to her car. My mother hopped up on one leg as I lifted her with the other man, and we shuffled together toward the sidewalk. We helped my mother sit against a concrete wall and I turned to watch the traffic roll again down the street.

I kneeled down and looked at my mother's hands, smudged black from the asphalt. Do we need to call an ambulance? I asked her. She opened her eyes and tried to slow her breathing. I don't think so, she said. Just let me sit. I looked up at the man and stood to take his hand. Gracias, I told him, not knowing what else to say. The man shook his head. It's nothing. In Juárez we take care of one another. He patted me on the back and gestured for me to sit down with my mother. When you're done here, he suggested, come visit my stand in the mercado. I'll be there with my mother, we'll make some quesadillas for the both of you. Before turning to leave he looked at me and raised his eyebrows. Aquí están en su casa.

I

In the dream I am hunched over in the darkness. The floor of the cave is covered with black shapes, arms and legs severed from the bodies that once carried them. I touch them and hold them in my hands, feeling dirt and blood and cold skin. I sort through the parts for a head, for the remnants of a face, for something to identify the people who were deposited here. I leave the cave empty-handed, emerging into a landscape devoid of color, the air still and raw. Outside, a voice tells me I must visit a wolf in a nearby cave. When I arrive there, little light is left in the sky. I walk through a stone passageway until I must squint to see through the darkness. At the back of the cave I can make out the rough shape of an animal circling in the shadows. Soon I discern the outline of a wolf walking slowly toward me, one paw placed silently before the next. As the animal approaches, my body swells with terror. I look over my shoulder and see the figure of my mother, gesturing for me to hold out my hand, to offer it to the wolf. I look forward and hold out my arm, breathing deeply as I open my palm. The wolf slowly comes near, stretching its neck to sniff my hand with its massive muzzle. The animal seems truly fearsome, but also wise. As it steps back to regard me, I sense that something is being communicated. The wolf approaches me again, this time standing slowly on its back legs and reaching for me, placing its paws on my chest. I am startled by the size of the paws, how heavy they feel against my chest. The wolf leans into me and brings its face close to mine, as if to tell me a secret. I close my eyes and feel its hot breath against my cheeks, its wet tongue on my face, licking the insides of my mouth. Then, suddenly, I awake.

We were on our way into town, speeding across the cold and brittle grasslands of New Mexico, when I heard about Santiago. Morales must have told me, or maybe it was Hart. I called Santiago as soon as I found out. You don't have to quit, I told him, you can still finish, you should stay. I can't, he said, it's not the work for me. I should go back to Puerto Rico, I should be with my family. I wished him luck and told him I was sorry to see him go. He thanked me and said to finish for the both of us, and I promised I would.

Of all my classmates, it was Santiago I most wanted to see graduate. He marched out of step, his gear was a mess, he couldn't handle his weapon, and it took him well over fifteen minutes to run the mile and a half. But he tried harder than any of us. He sweated the most, yelled the loudest. He was thirty-eight years old, an accountant from Puerto Rico, a husband and a recent father. The day before he quit, he left the firing range with a pocket full of live rounds and the instructors ordered him to sing "I'm a Little Teapot" in front of the class. He didn't know the song, so they suggested "God Bless America." He belted out the chorus at the top of his lungs, his chest heaving after each line as he gasped for air, thick with the smell of shit blowing in from the nearby dairy farms. We laughed, all of us, at his thick accent, at the misremembered verses, at his voice, off-key and quaking.

In town, over drinks, Hart went on about the winters in Detroit. I can't go back there, he said, not like Santiago. Fuck that. He glared down at his beer and then looked up at us. You know what I did before this? he asked. Morales and I shook our heads. I was a clerk at a rent-a-car desk in the goddamned airport. You know how many times I handed car keys to people who wouldn't even look me in the face? Guys who would glance at the tattoos on my arms like I was some thug, like I was some pathetic black kid part-timing outside the ghetto. Hart gripped his glass of beer. But more than any of that, I'm sick and tired of the winter.

Hart looked up from the table and mustered a smile. How about winter in Arizona? he asked. Morales laughed. You don't have to worry about snow where we're going, vato, that's for sure. Hart thought it sounded nice. Sure, I said, but wait until the summer. Have you ever felt 115-degree heat? Hell no, Hart answered. Well, I told him, we'll be out in it, fetching dead bodies from the desert. Hart looked puzzled. Who the fuck walks through the desert when it's 115? he asked. I drank through the final gulp of another beer. Migrants used to cross in the city, I told him, in places like San Diego and El Paso, until the Border Patrol shut it all down in the nineties with fences and new recruits like us. Politicians thought if they sealed the cities, people wouldn't risk crossing in the mountains and the deserts. But they were wrong, and now we're the ones who get to deal with it. Hart lost interest in my rambling and attempted to flag down the server to order another beer. Morales stared at the table and then glanced up at me, his eyes dark and buried beneath his brow. Sorry for the lecture, I told them. I studied this shit in school.

On our way back to the academy, I sat in the backseat of Morales's truck. In the front, Morales told Hart about growing up on the border in Douglas, about his uncles and cousins on the south side. Hart asked what kind of food they ate and Morales told him about hot bowls of menudo and birria in the morning, about the stands in Agua Prieta that sold tacos de tripa all through the night. Morales described how his mother made tortillas, how his grandmother prepared tamales at Christmastime, and I sat listening to his voice with my head against the cold glass of the window, staring at the darkened plain, slipping in and out of sleep.

ROBLES ORDERED US FROM THE MAT ROOM INTO THE SPINning room and we each took our place atop a stationary bicycle. At the front of the room, Robles climbed atop a machine that had been situated to face us and shouted for us to begin pedaling. At no point should your legs stop moving, he yelled. When I say stand, lift your ass off the seat and keep it in the air until I tell you to sit. He snapped his head toward a stout man in the front row named Hanson. Is that clear, Mr. Hanson? Yes sir, Hanson shouted, already out of breath.

As the minutes passed, Robles prodded us to work harder—sit, he shouted, move those legs, stand. Your body is a tool, he announced, the most important one you have. A baton is nothing, a Taser is nothing, even your gun is nothing if you give up on your body when it becomes tired, if you can't hold it together when every muscle cries out for you to quit. In the Border Patrol, Robles continued, you will be tested—I can promise you that. In my time, I have taken a life and I have saved a life. When I was brand-new to the field, like all of you will be, my journeyman and I jumped a group of El Sals in the lettuce fields outside Yuma. A man ran from us and I chased after him until I thought my legs would give out. I stumbled and tripped over dirt berms and rows of lettuce, but I kept chasing him until we came to the edge of a canal and the man turned to face me. He came at me before I could react and we went to the ground fighting. If I had given up, maybe the man would have killed me. But I didn't. I grappled with him in the dirt until I knocked him over the edge of the canal into the water. The man couldn't swim, none of them can, and so an hour later me and my journeyman fished his dead body out of the water at a buoy line.

Robles's eyes seemed to detach from his surroundings, as if his gaze had turned inward. A year after that, he continued, I chased another man to the banks of the Colorado River. He ran out into the water and was swept away by the current like it was nothing. And I'll tell you what I did. I swam into the river and I battled to keep him afloat even as I inhaled mouthfuls of water, even though I can't remember ever having been more tired. I saved that man's life, and still, there's not a single day I don't think about the one I took before it.

As Robles fell silent, we stood sweating over our bikes, our legs pedaling weakly. In the front row, Hanson dropped his head, his ass falling to the seat. Robles snapped his gaze from the middle of the room and turned his head toward Hanson. Get back up there, he roared. Don't give up on me, Mr. Hanson. Do not give up.

As the sound of our labored breathing settled back over the room, I thought briefly of the man from El Salvador and wondered how the news of his death might have arrived to his family, floating in the air like a corpse in black water. At the front of the room I watched Robles standing tall atop his bicycle, sweat dripping from his brow as he thrust his shoulders downward with each stroke of his legs. I wondered at his unwavering exertion, if his body was still being driven to make good for the life he had seen blink out in the swift currents of the canal. I wondered if he thought of his body as a tool for destruction or as one of safekeeping. I wondered, too, about my body, about what sort of tool it was becoming.

BEFORE WE TOOK TO THE RANGE ONE AFTERNOON, THE firearms instructor gave the class a PowerPoint presentation in a darkened room. Agents arrested more than 700,000 aliens on the border last year, he told us. If you think that's bad, when I first got to the field eight years ago, back in 2000, that number was over one and a half million. And I'm here to tell you that not everybody coming across that line is a good person looking for honest work.

Our instructor beamed images of drug war victims onto a screen, grisly photos of people killed by the cartels in Mexico. In one image, three heads floated in a massive ice chest. In another, a woman's body lay discarded in the desert, her feet bound, a severed hand stuffed into her mouth. The instructor paused on an image of a cattle truck with twelve dead bodies stacked in the back, all of them blindfolded and shot execution-style. These twelve weren't gangsters, he told us, they were migrants kidnapped and killed for some meager and meaningless ransom. The next image showed a group of Mexican policemen shot dead in the street, and then an image of a bloodied body slumped in a car seat—a newly elected mayor who had promised to clean up the drug violence in his town, shot dead on his first day in office.

This is what you're up against, our instructor told us, this is what's coming.

SO FAR SEVEN HAVE QUIT, WHITTLING OUR CLASS DOWN TO forty-three. Sullivan left exactly one week after Santiago. I didn't know him but his roommate said he complained a lot. Serra, one of only three women in the class, quit two days later and no one knew why. She kept to herself, everyone said. Golinski went next, taking indefinite medical leave for a hairline fracture around his left knee. When I saw him at the computer lab the night before he left, I asked him what he would do when he got back home. He looked at me as if he didn't understand the question. I'll wait for my knee to heal and come back to the academy, he told me. I've had two tours in Iraq—I know I can do this job.

Hanson quit after receiving a job offer from his hometown police department in Illinois. It pays almost as well, he told us, and I won't have to move my wife and kids. On Hanson's last day at the academy, Robles lined us up at the start of PT and had us stand shirtless while he measured our body fat percentage. Hanson stood next to me in formation and I saw for the first time the loose skin that hung from his waist. When Robles came to take his measurements he glanced at the extra skin and then up at Hanson's face. How much weight did you lose? Robles asked. A hundred eighty pounds in a year and a half, Hanson said, staring straight ahead. Robles nodded. Let's hope you never put it back on.

Dominguez, Hart's roommate, was next to quit, dropping out after failing his third law test. For days I wondered if I could have done more to help him pass. One night Hart and I sat eating dinner together at a cafeteria table. Why didn't you invite him to study with us? I asked. He was your roommate, you should have looked after him. Hart looked at me incredulously. Fuck you, he said, tossing his dinner roll onto his plate. Dominguez could have passed if he wanted to. He was too busy talking on the fucking phone all night. Listen, he said, Dominguez was smart enough to pass the U.S. citizenship test in high school and he was smart enough to earn a bachelor's degree in construction management after that. You're not the only one who went to college. Hell, he was even smart enough to run his own construction business before the housing market went to shit, did you know that? Hart picked the dinner roll off his plate and ripped off a bite. Instead of studying, he continued, Dominguez spent all his free time talking to his family, and it's sure as hell not my fault or anyone else's. I sat thinking for several moments. What did they talk about? I finally asked. Hart shrugged his shoulders. How should I know, he said, I don't speak Spanish.

MY MOTHER FLEW IN FROM ARIZONA TO SEE ME FOR CHRIST-mas. She picked me up from the academy on Christmas Eve and we drove through the straw-colored hills, leaving behind the trembling Chihuahuan grasslands as we climbed into evergreen mountains. We stayed the night in a two-room cabin, warm and bright with pinewood. We sat in chairs around the living room table, decorating a miniature tree with tiny glass bulbs. Then, wrapped in blankets, we laughed and drank eggnog with brandy until the conversation finally descended into a discussion of my impending work.

Listen, my mother said, I spent most of my career as a park ranger, so I've got nothing against you working for the government. But don't you think it's sort of below you, earning a degree just to become a border cop? When people ask about you back home and I tell them you're in law enforcement, they give me the strangest looks. I realize I don't know what more to tell them, I don't really understand what you want from this work.

I took a deep breath. Look, I told her, I spent four years in college studying international relations and learning about the border through policy and history. You can tell whoever asks that I'm tired of studying, I'm tired of reading about the border in books. I want

22

to be on the ground, out in the field, I want to see the realities of the border day in and day out. I know it might be ugly, I know it might be dangerous, but I don't see any better way to truly understand the place.

My mother stared at me, blinking rapidly. Are you crazy? she asked. There are a hundred other ways of knowing a place. You grew up near the border, living with me in deserts and national parks. The border is in our blood, for Christ's sake—your great-grandparents brought my father across from Mexico when he was just a little boy. When I married, I insisted on keeping my maiden name so that you'd always carry something from your grandfather's family, so you'd never forget your heritage. How's that for knowing the border?

I lowered my voice. I'm grateful for those things, I told her, but having a name isn't the same as understanding a place. I gestured toward the window. I want to be outside. Not in a classroom, not in an office, not sitting at a computer, not staring at papers. Do you remember, I asked my mother, how you joined the Park Service because you wanted to be outdoors, because you felt you could understand yourself in wild places? My mother narrowed her eyes at me as if I had suddenly changed the subject. It's not that different, I said. I don't know if the border is a place for me to understand myself, but I know there's something here I can't look away from. Maybe it's the desert, maybe it's the closeness of life and death, maybe it's the tension between the two cultures we carry inside us. Whatever it is, I'll never understand it unless I'm close to it.

My mother shook her head. You make it sound like you'll be communing with nature and having heartfelt conversations all day. The Border Patrol isn't the Park Service. It's a paramilitary police force. I glared at her. You don't have to tell me that, I said—I'm the one getting my ass kicked at the academy.

Listen, I know you don't want your only son turning into a heartless cop. I know you're afraid the job will turn me into someone brutal and callous. Those people who look at you funny when you tell them I'm in the Border Patrol probably imagine an agency full of white racists out to kill and deport Mexicans. But that's not me, and those aren't the kind of people I see at the academy. Nearly half my classmates are Hispanic—some of them grew up speaking Spanish, some grew up right on the border. Some went to college, like me. Some went to war, some owned businesses, some worked dead-end jobs, some are fresh out of high school. Some are fathers and mothers with their own children. These people aren't joining the Border Patrol to oppress others. They're joining because it represents an opportunity for service, stability, financial security—

My mother interrupted me. But you could work anywhere you want, she said, you graduated with honors.

So what? I asked. This isn't necessarily a lifelong career choice. Think of it as another part of my education. Imagine what I'll learn—imagine the perspective I'll gain. Look, I know you're not an enforcement-minded person, but the reality of the border is one of enforcement. I might not agree with every aspect of U.S. border policy, but there is power in understanding the realities it creates.

Maybe after three or four years I'll go back to school to study law, maybe I'll work to shape new policies. If I become an immigration lawyer or a policy maker, imagine the unique knowledge I'll bring, imagine how much better I'll be at the job because of my time in the Border Patrol.

My mother sighed and looked up at the ceiling. There are ways to learn these things that don't put you at risk, she said, ways that let you help people instead of pitting you against them. But that's just it, I offered—I can still help people. I speak both languages, I know both cultures. I've lived in Mexico and traveled all across the country. I've seen towns and villages that were emptied out by people going north for work. Good people will always be crossing the border, and whether I'm in the Border Patrol or not, agents will be out there arresting them. At least if I'm the one apprehending them, I can offer them some small comfort by speaking with them in their own language, by talking to them with knowledge of their home.

Fine, my mother said, fine. But you must understand you are stepping into a system, an institution with little regard for people.

I looked away from her and a silence hung between us. I glanced down at my hands and weighed my mother's words. Maybe you're right, I replied, but stepping into a system doesn't mean that the system becomes you. As I spoke, doubts flickered through my mind. I smiled at my mother. The first job I ever had was bussing dishes with migrants from Guanajuato, I reminded her. I'm not going to lose sight of that. I'm not going to become someone else.

Good, my mother said. I hope you're right.

We hugged, and my mother told me she loved me, that she was happy I'd soon be working back in Arizona, closer to her. Before bed, we each opened a single present, as we had done every Christmas Eve since I could remember.

In the morning we ate brunch at the town's historic hotel, feasting on pot roast by a crackling fire. Afterward we climbed the stairs to a narrow lookout tower where people huddled together in jackets, walking in slow circles to take in the view. Below us, a sunlit basin stretched westward from the base of the mountains. I watched as the landscape shifted under the winter light. Behind me, my mother placed her hand on my shoulder and pointed to a cloud of gypsum sand in the distance, impossibly small, swirling across the desert below.

AT GRADUATION WE STOOD BEFORE FRIENDS AND LOVED ones in our campaign hats and full-dress uniforms with iron-creased pant legs and shirtsleeves, our boots and brass buckles polished to shine under the fluorescent light of the academy's auditorium. Our instructors made speeches about the value of our training, about the importance of our pending duties. We received awards, badges were pinned to our chests. We stood side by side and turned to face our audience, holding up our right hands as we stared steely-eyed at the room's pale walls. I do solemnly swear that I will support and defend the Constitution of the United States against all enemies, foreign and domestic; that I will bear true faith and allegiance to the same; that I take this obligation freely, without any mental reservation or purpose of evasion; and that I will well and faithfully discharge the duties of the office on which I am about to enter. So help me God.

WE CAUGHT OUR FIRST DOPE LOAD ONLY TWO DAYS AFTER arriving at the station. We were east of the port of entry when a sensor hit, just three miles away. At the trailhead, Cole, our supervisor, pointed to a mess of footprints stamped in the dirt. He followed the prints up the trail and after several minutes motioned for us to pile out of the vehicles. We've got foot sign for eight, he told us, keep quiet and follow me.

For five miles we walked toward the mountains with Cole leading the way. He called us up one by one to watch us cut the sign. Keep your vision soft, he told us, scan the ground about five or six yards out. Try to cut with the sun in front of you, never at your back, so that the sign catches the light. If a trail gets hard to cut, look for small disturbances—toe digs, heel prints, kicked-over rocks, the shine of pressed-in dirt, fibers snagged on spines and branches. If you lose the sign, go back to where you last had it. Learn to read the dirt, he said, it's your bread and butter.

We found the first bundle discarded among the boulders at the base of the pass. They must have seen us coming, Cole said. He directed us to spread out to comb the hillsides, and after ten minutes we had recovered two backpacks filled with food and clothes and four additional bundles wrapped in sugar sacks spray-painted black. Those ought to be about fifty pounds each, Cole told us. He kicked one of the bundles with his foot. Two hundred fifty pounds of dope—not bad for your second day in the field. I asked Cole if we should follow the foot sign up into the pass, if we should try to track down the backpackers. Hell no, he said, you don't want to bring in any bodies with your dope if you can help it. Suspects mean you have a smuggling case on your hands, and that's a hell of a lot of paperwork—we'd have to stay and work a double shift just to write it up. Besides, he said, the prosecutors won't take it anyway. Courts here are flooded with cases like this. He smiled. Abandoned loads are easy though. You'll see.

Cole had us dump the backpacks and I watched as several of my classmates ripped and tore at the clothing, scattering it among the tangled branches of mesquite and palo verde. In one of the backpacks I found a laminated prayer card depicting Saint Jude, a tongue of flames hovering above his head. Morales found a pack of cigarettes and sat smoking on a rock as others laughed loudly and stepped on a heap of food. Nearby, Hart giggled and shouted to us as he pissed on a pile of ransacked belongings.

As we hiked with the bundles back to our vehicles, the February sun grew low in the sky and cast a warm light over the desert. At the edge of the trail, in the pink shade of a palo verde, a desert tortoise raised itself on its front legs to watch us pass.

AT NIGHT WE STOOD FOR HOURS IN THE DARKNESS ALONG the pole line. After we had tired of the cold and the buzzing power lines, Cole had us lay a spike strip across the dirt road and return to wait in our vehicles, parked in a nearby wash. We sat with the engines on and the heat blasting, and after a few minutes of silence, Morales asked Cole why some of the agents at the station called him "Black Death." Cole laughed and pulled a can of Copenhagen from his shirt pocket. You have to be careful, he said, the Indians out here, when they're drunk and walking at night between the villages, they fall asleep on the fucking road. He packed the can as he spoke, swinging his right arm and thumping his forefinger across the lid. When it's cold out, the asphalt holds warmth from the sun, even at night. A few years ago I was working the midnight shift, driving down IR-9, and I saw this fucking Indian asleep in the middle of the road. I stopped the truck and woke his ass up. His brother was there with him, sleeping in the bushes. They were drunk as hell. Cole pinched a wad of dip into his mouth. His lower lip bulged, catching the green light from the control panel. I gave the guys a ride into the next village, he said, dropped them off at their cousin's place. Told them not to sleep on the goddamn road. He grabbed an empty Pepsi cup from the center console and spat. Maybe nine or ten months later, same fucking spot, I ran over the guy, killed him right there. Same fucking guy, asleep on the damn road. I never even saw him.

After that, they started calling me Black Death. Cole laughed and spat into his cup and a few of us laughed with him, not knowing exactly what kind of laugh it was.

Just after midnight a blacked-out truck roared across the spikes and three of its tires went. We tore after it, speeding blindly through a cloud of dust until we realized the vehicle had turned. We doubled back to where the tire sign left the road and followed it until we came upon the truck abandoned at the foot of a hill. In the back of the truck we found two marijuana bundles and a .22 rifle. Cole sent us to scour the hillside with our flashlights, but we recovered only one other bundle. It's a fucking gimme load, Cole said. I asked what he meant. It's a goddamn distraction, that's what. They're waiting us out. But my classmates and I didn't care—we were high from the chase. We drove the truck into a wash until it became stuck, and we slashed the unpopped tire, leaving it there with the lights on and the engine running. On the way back to the station I asked Cole what would happen to the truck. He told me he'd call the tribal police to seize the vehicle, but I knew he wouldn't. Even if he did, they wouldn't come for it. They wouldn't want the paperwork either.

AFTER SUNDOWN COLE SENT MORALES UP A HILL NEAR THE highway with a thermal reconnaissance camera. Let me borrow your beanie, vato, he said to me, it's cold out. I handed it to him and stayed inside the vehicle with the others. An hour later Morales spotted a group of ten just east of mile marker five. We rushed out of the car and set out on foot as he guided us in on the radio, but by the time we got there the group had already scattered. We found them one by one, huddled in the brush and curled up around the trunks of palo verde trees and cholla cactus. Not one of them ran. We made them take off their shoelaces and empty their backpacks and we walked all ten of them single file back to the road. For a while I walked next to an older man who told me they were all from Michoacán. It's beautiful there, I said. Yes, he replied, but there's no work. You've been to Michoacán? he asked. I told him I had. Then you must have seen what it's like to live in Mexico, he said. And now you see what it's like for us at the border. We walked on, and then, after several minutes, he sighed deeply. Hay mucha desesperación, he told me, almost whispering. I tried to look at his face, but it was too dark.

At the station I processed the man for deportation. After I had taken his fingerprints he asked me if there was any work for him at the station. You don't understand, I said, you've just got to wait here until the bus comes. They'll take you to headquarters and then on to the border. You'll be back in Mexico very soon. I understand, he assured me, I just want to know if there is something I can do while I wait, something to help. I can take out the trash or clean out the cells. I want to show you that I'm here to work, that I'm not a bad person. I'm not here to bring in drugs, I'm not here to do anything illegal. I want to work. I looked at him. I know that, I said.

COLE TOOK US TO A LAY-UP SPOT JUST OFF THE HIGHWAY where he had almost been run over by smugglers. He led us to a wide wash full of old blankets and discarded clothes and pieces of twine and empty cans of tuna and crushed water bottles. We climbed out of the wash and walked up to a nearby cactus, a tall and sprawling chain-fruit cholla, and Cole asked if any of us had hand sanitizer. Someone tossed him a small bottle and he emptied the gel on the black trunk of the cactus. He asked for a lighter and with it he lit the gel, then stepped back to watch the flames crawl up the trunk, crackling and popping as they engulfed the plant's spiny arms. In the light from the fire, Cole packed his can of dip and took a pinch into his mouth. His bottom lip shone taut and smooth, his shaved black skin reflecting the light from the flames. He spat into the fire and the rest of us stood with him in a circle around the cholla as it burned, laughing and taking pictures and videos with our phones as thick smoke billowed into the night, filling the air with the resinous smell of hot asphalt.

COLE WAS AHEAD SCOUTING THE TRAIL IN THE DARKNESS when he radioed to us about the mountain lion. Come with your sidearms drawn, he said. We figured he was fucking with us. We were talking loudly, walking with our flashlights on—surely a mountain lion would shy away. We continued down the trail until the ground leveled off and it was then that a sharp hiss issued up from the darkness beside us, a sound like hot wind escaping the depths of the earth. Holy fucking shit, we said. We drew our side-arms and shuffled down the path back-to-back, casting light in all directions. I felt a profound and immediate fear—not of the danger posed to us by the animal, but of the idea that it might show itself to us, so many men armed and heedless.

THERE ARE DAYS WHEN I FEEL I AM BECOMING GOOD AT what I do. And then I wonder, what does it mean to be good at this? I wonder sometimes how I might explain certain things, the sense in what we do when they run from us, scattering into the brush, leaving behind their water jugs and their backpacks full of food and clothes, how to explain what we do when we discover their lay-up spots stocked with water and stashed rations. Of course, what you do depends on who you're with, depends on what kind of agent you are, what kind of agent you want to become, but it's true that we slash their bottles and drain their water into the dry earth, that we dump their backpacks and pile their food and clothes to be crushed and pissed on and stepped over, strewn across the desert and set ablaze. And Christ, it sounds terrible, and maybe it is, but the idea is that when they come out from their hiding places, when they regroup and return to find their stockpiles ransacked and stripped, they'll realize their situation, that they're fucked, that it's hopeless to continue, and they'll quit right then and there, they'll save themselves and struggle toward the nearest highway or dirt road to flag down some passing agent or they'll head for the nearest parched village to knock on someone's door, someone who will give them food and water and call us to take them in—that's the idea, the sense in it all. But still, I have nightmares, visions of them staggering through the desert, men from Michoacán, from places I've known, men lost and wandering without food or water, dying slowly as they look for some road, some village, some way out. In my dreams I seek them out, searching in vain until finally I discover their bodies lying facedown on the ground before me, dead and stinking on the desert floor, human waypoints in a vast and smoldering expanse.

IN 1706 THE ITALIAN PRIEST FATHER EUSEBIO KINO CLIMBED to the summit of a volcanic peak just south of the international boundary line that would come, nearly 150 years later, to separate the territory of the United States from the contiguous lands of Mexico. From this vantage point, he looked out across a massive dune field and hardened flows of black lava, all the way to the glistening blue arc of the Gulf of California. It was then that Father Kino, the first white man to reach this high and isolated place, recognized what the native people of this desert had long known: that the landmass of Baja California was not the island that conquerors and missionaries had always assumed it to be, but was in fact connected to the rest of the North American continent, a narrow peninsula reaching down into ancient and teeming waters. Across the pale sands and shimmering sea, Father Kino could make out the mouth of the Colorado River and the wooded peaks of Sierra de San Pedro Mártir, the peninsula's highest range.

Down in the dune field, Father Kino encountered a wandering people. They cleared long strips of dry ground for ceremonies and traced massive figures onto the surface of the earth, human and animal shapes scraped into the desert pavement and lined with carefully placed stones. For untold centuries they had inhabited a landscape of craters, collapsed calderas, and jagged mountains half buried by sand. They met with few other peoples, occasionally trading goods with neighboring tribes and granting passage to those who journeyed across their parched lands on pilgrimages to collect salt at the nearby edges of the sea.

To Father Kino these people were feeble and ragged, barely surviving on a diet of roots and lizards. But they understood that there was life to be had in the desert, a life worth struggling for. To the Europeans the entire region was a malpaís, a bad country, but those who made their lives there knew it as a place inextricable from the terrain that surrounded it, a single unbroken expanse.

AFTER THREE MONTHS WE WERE FINALLY RELEASED FROM the training unit and dispersed into rotating shifts to work under journeymen agents. I was sent to midnights and partnered with Mortenson, a four-year veteran of the patrol. I'll tell you what, Mortenson said to me on our first shift together, it throws me for a loop every time they assign me to be a journeyman. Seems like just yesterday I was a trainee myself. My first journeyman was salty as shit, Mortenson scoffed. He kept going on about the "old patrol" and the "new patrol," about how nobody with less than eight years in the field should be a journeyman. But that was before the big hiring push—there's so many people coming in and out of the station nowadays that even junior agents move up fast. Mortenson smiled. So here I am, your very own journeyman.

Listen, don't worry about calling me sir or any of that bullshit. He looked over at me as he drove us down the highway. My old man is the hardest-ass cop you'll ever meet, made me call him sir ever since I can remember. Shit, I'm twenty-three years old and all I've ever known is law enforcement. Mortenson stared out into the darkness beyond his headlights. What about you? he asked. I'm twenty-three too, I told him. Well there you go, he said, the last thing I need is a dude my own age calling me sir. But hell, he smirked, I'll let you wash the ride at the end of the shift.

Early one morning, before dawn, Mortenson brought me to the port of entry. It's smart to make friends with the customs agents, he told me—they keep their eye on the foot traffic and the vehicles that cross through the port, and we take care of everything in between. If you get these guys to like you, sometimes they'll throw you some good intel. He introduced me to a supervisor and got permission for us to monitor the video feeds in the camera room. For nearly an hour we watched a grid of dimly lit buildings and roads surrounding the port until the sun slowly began to rise outside, bleeding warmth onto the screens. Mortenson pointed toward a monitor in the far-left corner and we watched as the pixelated figures of two men and a woman cut a hole in the pedestrian fence. We bolted from the room and ran to the site of the breach, rounding the corner just in time to see the men already scrambling back through the hole to Mexico. The woman stood motionless beside the fence, too scared to run.

As Mortenson inspected the breach, the girl wept beside me, telling me it was her birthday, that she was turning twenty-three, pleading for me to let her go and swearing she would never cross again. Mortenson turned and took a long look at the woman and laughed. I booked her last week, he said. She spoke hurriedly to us as we walked back to the port of entry and while Mortenson went inside to gather our things I stood with her in the parking lot. She told me she was from Guadalajara, that she had some problems there, that she had already tried four times to cross. She swore to me that she would stay in Mexico for good this time, that she would finally go back to finish music school. Te lo juro, she said. She looked at me and smiled. Someday I'm going to be a singer, you know. I believe it, I said, smiling back. She told me that she thought I was nice, and before Mortenson returned from the port she snuck her counterfeit green card into my hand. I don't want to get in trouble at the processing center like last time, she said. I looked toward the port of entry and slipped the card into my pocket. When Mortenson came back we helped her into the patrol vehicle and drove north toward the station, laughing and applauding as she sang "Bidi Bidi

Bom Bom" to us from the backseat. She's going to be a singer, I told Mortenson. The woman beamed. Shit, he said. She already is.

AT NIGHT, FINALLY ALLOWED TO PATROL ON MY OWN, I SAT watching storms roll across the moonlit desert. There were three of them: the first due south in Mexico, the second creeping down from the mountains in the east, and the third hovering just behind me— close enough for me to feel smatterings of rain and gusts of warm wind. In the distance lightning appeared like a line of hot neon, illuminating the desert in a shuddering white light.

AT THE STATION I WAS GIVEN THE KEYS TO A TRANSPORT van and told to drive out to the reservation where two quitters had been seen wandering through the streets of a small village. When I arrived it was just after dark and I noticed few signs of life as I drove past the scattered homes, scanning for disheartened crossers. In the center of the village a small adobe church stood in an empty dirt lot, and I saw that the front door had been left ajar. I parked the van and left the headlights shining on the entrance. I walked to the heavy wooden door and leaned with all my weight to push it open, caus- ing a loud and violent scraping to rise up and echo into the dim interior.

Inside the church, the light from my flashlight glinted off tiny strings of tinsel hanging from the ceiling. A large piece of fabric depicting the Virgin of Guadalupe was strung across the front wall, and beneath it I saw two figures lying on a blanket that had been spread out between the pews and the altar. As I approached, a man looked up at me and squinted, holding out his hand to block the light. We were resting a little, he said. It's just that we are lost, muy desanimados. A woman huddled close to him, hiding her face. The man propped himself up on one elbow and told me that they had crossed four days ago, that their guide had left them behind on the first night when they'd failed to keep pace with the group. They were lost for days, he said, with nothing to drink but the filthy water from cattle tanks. Puede ser muy fea la frontera, I told him. The man shook his head. Pues sí, he replied, pero es aún más feo donde nosotros vivimos.

The man told me that they came from Morelos. My wife and I, we're just coming to find work, he said. He rubbed his eyes in silence. I have fresh water for you, I told them. At the station there's juice and crackers. The man looked at me and smiled weakly, then asked for a minute to gather their belongings. He stuffed some things into a backpack, then helped his wife to her feet. Her face was streaked with dried tears, and when she turned toward me I saw that she was pregnant. How many months are you? I asked. The woman looked away and the man answered for her. Seis meses. He smiled. My wife speaks perfect English, he said, shouldering the backpack. He stopped in front of the altar, bowing his head and making the sign of the cross. I waited at the door as he mumbled a prayer. Gracias, he whispered. Gracias.

Outside I looked at their faces in the glare of my headlights. The woman seemed young. Where did you learn English? I asked. Iowa, she told me quietly. I grew up there, she said, I even got my GED. She kept her head down and avoided my gaze as she talked, glancing up only briefly at my uniformed body. Why did you leave? I asked her. She told me that she had returned to Morelos to care for her younger siblings after their mother died. In Morelos I made some money teaching English at the kindergarten, she said, I even tutored the adults in my village, people preparing for the journey north. For a few seconds she seemed proud, and then she shook her head. But the money there, it isn't enough. She glanced up at her husband. It was my idea to cross, she said. I wanted our child to have a life here, like I did.

The man took a moment to look at me in the light. Listen, he said, do you think you could bring us back to Mexico, como hermano? You could drive us down to the border, he pleaded, you could just leave us there, allí en la línea. Like a brother. I sighed and turned my head, squinting at the darkness beyond the church. I have to bring you in, I told him. It's my job. The man took a deep breath and nodded and then climbed into the back of the transport van, holding out his arms to help his pregnant wife.

I gestured at a case of water bottles on the floor. You should drink, I told them. I grabbed the metal door of the cage and paused. What are your names? I asked. The man looked at me strangely and glanced at his wife. Then, as if it were nothing, they took turns introducing themselves. I repeated their names and I told them mine.

Mucho gusto, I said. They replied with polite smiles. Igualmente. I turned my head and then bolted the cage and shut the door.

In the driver's seat I turned to look at the couple through the plexiglass. The man held his wife and gently whispered to her, cradling her head. Just before I started the engine I could hear the soft sound of her sobbing. As I drove through the unmarked streets of the village, trying to find my way to the highway, I felt for a moment that I had become lost. Beyond the last house, I saw a white dog in the darkness at the edge of my headlights, staring into the night.

At the station, I sorted through their things with them, discarding perishables and sharp objects. I had them remove their belts and their shoelaces and I tagged their backpacks and handed them a claim ticket. I counted and took note of their money, in pesos and in dollars, and then handed it back to them, telling them to keep it close. Inside the processing center I filled out their voluntary return papers and entered their names into the computer. Before leaving them in their cell I wished them luck on their journey and asked them to be safe, to always think of their child.

Later that night, as I sat in the transport van listening to the calls come out over the radio, I realized I had forgotten their names.

THE MODERN-DAY BOUNDARY BETWEEN THE UNITED STATES and Mexico was defined largely by the Treaty of Guadalupe Hidalgo in 1848, signed after nearly two years of warfare between neighboring republics. The newly agreed-upon borderline was to begin "on the coast of the Pacific Ocean, distant one marine league due south of the southernmost point of the port of San Diego," and run east "following the division line between Upper and Lower California" until it reached the Colorado River at the town of Yuma. The treaty dictated that the line would then follow the course of the Gila River from its intersection with the Colorado until it reached the border of New Mexico, at which point the boundary would leave the waters of the Gila in a straight line until it intersected the Rio Grande north of El Paso, where the line would again become fluid "following the deepest channel" of the river until it emptied into the Gulf of Mexico, to be forgotten in the waters of the ocean at a point "three leagues from land, opposite the mouth of the Rio Grande."

Article V of the treaty mandated that "in order to designate the boundary line with due precision, upon authoritative maps, and to establish upon the ground landmarks which shall show the limits of both Republics . . . the two Governments shall each appoint a commissioner and a surveyor, who . . . shall meet at the port of San Diego, and proceed to run and mark the said boundary in its whole course to the mouth of the Rio Bravo del Norte." It added that "the boundary line established by this article shall be religiously respected by each of the two Republics."

Following the ratification of the treaty, both countries appointed commissioners and surveyors to mark the new boundary. The surveying was initially carried out under the questionable supervision of John Russell Bartlett, a well-connected and adventure-hungry bookseller living in New York. After many fits and starts, the commission established the initial point of the boundary on the Pacific coast and marked it with a "substantial monument," and made a similar determination "at the junction of the Gila and Colorado rivers, where another monument was placed." Between these two points, the commission marked the boundary with five intermediate monuments.

Several years later, in 1853, the boundary line was modified by the Treaty of La Mesilla, commonly known in the United States as the Gadsden Purchase. Instead of following the natural course of the Gila River across Arizona to the edge of New Mexico, the new agreement stipulated that a rigid and pivoting line would dip south from Yuma and run east to the Rio Grande, adding nearly thirty thousand square miles of territory to the southern edges of Arizona and New Mexico.

In the first article of the new agreement, it was stated that each government would again nominate a commissioner whose duty it would be "to survey and mark out upon the land the dividing line stipulated by this article, where it shall not have already been surveyed and established." Over the course of three years following the treaty's ratification, a new survey was undertaken that included many personnel from the original commission. The newly appointed commissioner, William H. Emory, brought great conviction to his work, deeming it "fortunate that two nations, which differ so much in laws, religion, customs, and physical wants, should be separated by lines." While he regretted that the new boundary should limit the "inevitable expansive force" of the United States, he

FRANCISCO CANTÚ

nevertheless declared with characteristic zeal that "no line traversing the continent could probably be found which is better suited to
the purpose."

In the course of their work along the international boundary,
Emory's surveying parties erected, in addition to the six still-suitable
monuments previously established along California's border with
Mexico, the placement of forty-seven monuments along the newly
traced line from the Colorado River to the Rio Grande, asserting,
for the very first time, the entirety of a boundary that had hitherto
existed only on paper and in the furious minds of politicians.

AGENTS FOUND MARTIN UBALDE DE LA VEGA AND HIS THREE
companions on the bombing range more than fifty miles north of
the border. The four men had been in the desert for six days and had
wandered in the July heat for over forty-eight hours without food or
water. By the time of rescue, one of the men had already met his
death. Of the survivors, one was quickly treated and discharged
from the hospital, while another remained in intensive care, recently awoken from a coma, unable to remember his own name.
When I arrived at the hospital asking for the third survivor, nurses
explained that he was recovering from kidney failure and guided me
to his room, where he lay hidden like a dark stone in white sheets.

I had been charged with watching over de la Vega until his condition was stable, at which point I would transport him to the station to
be processed for deportation. I settled in a chair next to him, and after

several minutes of silence, I asked him to tell me about himself. He answered timidly, as if unsure of what to say or even how to speak. He apologized for his Spanish, explaining that he knew only what they had taught him in school. He came from the jungles of Guerrero, he told me, and in his village they spoke Mixtec and farmed the green earth. He was the father of seven children, he said, five girls and two boys. His eldest daughter lived in California and he had crossed the border with plans to go there, to live with her and find work.

We spent the following hours watching telenovelas and occasionally he would turn to ask me about the women in America, wondering if they were like the ones on TV. He began to tell me about his youngest daughter, still in Mexico. She's just turned eighteen, he said. You could marry her.

Later that afternoon, de la Vega was cleared for release. The nurse brought in his belongings—a pair of blue jeans and sneakers with holes worn through the soles. I asked what had happened to his shirt. I don't know, he answered. I looked at the nurse and she shrugged, telling me he had come in that way. We've got no clothes here, she added, only hospital gowns. As we exited through the hospital lobby, I watched the way eyes fell across his shirtless body. I imagined him alone and half naked in the days to come as he was ferried through alien territory, booked and transferred between government processing centers and finally bused to the border to reenter his country.

In the parking lot I placed him in the passenger seat of my patrol vehicle and popped the trunk. At the back of the cruiser I unbuckled my gun belt, unbuttoned my uniform shirt, and removed my white V-neck. I reassembled my uniform and returned to the passenger door to offer him my undershirt.

Before leaving town, I asked him if he was hungry. You should eat something now, I told him, at the station there's only juice and crackers. I asked what he was hungry for. What do Americans eat? he asked. I laughed. Here we eat mostly Mexican food. He looked at me unbelievingly. But we also eat hamburgers, I said. We pulled into a McDonald's and at the drive-through window de la Vega turned to me and told me he didn't have any money. Yo te invito, I said.

As we drove south along the open highway, I tuned in to a Mexican radio station and we listened to the sounds of norteño as he ate his meal. After finishing he sat silently next to me, watching the passing desert. Then, as if whispering to me or to someone else, he began to speak of the rains in Guerrero, of the wet and green jungle, and I wondered if he could ever have been made to imagine a place like this—a place where one of his companions would meet his death and another would be made to forget his own name, a landscape where the earth still seethed with volcanic heat.

AS I CUT FOR SIGN ALONG THE BORDER ROAD, I WATCHED A Sonoran coachwhip snake try to find its way into Mexico through the pedestrian fence. The animal slithered along the length of the mesh looking for a way south, hitting its head against the rusted metal again and again until finally I guided it over to the wide opening of a wash grate. After the snake had made its way across the adjacent road, I stood for a while looking through the mesh, staring at the undulating tracks left in the dirt.

A WOMAN ON THE SOUTH SIDE OF THE PEDESTRIAN FENCE flagged me down as I passed her on the border road. I stopped my vehicle and went over to her. With panic in her voice she asked me if I knew about her son—he had crossed days ago, she said, or maybe it was a week ago, she wasn't sure. She hadn't heard anything from him, no one had, and she didn't know if he had been caught or if he was lost somewhere in the desert or if he was even still alive. Estamos desesperados, she told me, her voice quivering, with one hand clawing at her chest and the other trembling against the fence. I don't remember what I told her, if I took down the man's name or if I gave her the phone number to some faraway office or hotline, but I remember thinking later about de la Vega, about his dead and delirious companions, about all the questions I should have asked the woman. I arrived home that evening and threw my gun belt and uniform across the couch. Standing alone in my empty living room, I called my mother. I'm safe, I told her, I'm home.

THREE DECADES AFTER SIGNING THE TREATY OF LA MESILLA, successive conventions of Mexican and United States diplomats convened in Washington, D.C., in 1882, 1884, and again in 1889, to discuss the state of the boundary between the two nations. In the years since the last boundary commission had concluded its work in 1856, settlers had been moving to the southwest in growing numbers to work on landholdings and newly discovered mines adjacent to the international border. In many places, the exact location of the boundary had become a matter of contentious debate, presenting great difficulty to government authorities on both sides of the line. In some cases, it was even charged that quarreling parties had destroyed or removed the boundary markers that had been erected at great cost to both countries in the previous decades.

During the course of these binational meetings, representatives of both countries agreed on the pressing need to determine "(a) the condition of the present boundary monuments; (b) the number of destroyed or displaced monuments; (c) the places, settled or capable of eventual settlement, where it may be advisable to set the monuments closer together along the line than at present; (d) the character of the new monuments required, whether of stone or iron; and their number, approximately, in each case." The conventions thus called for the establishment of a new international boundary commission, which was to possess the power and authority to reposition incorrectly placed or missing monuments, "to erect new monuments on the site of former monuments when these shall have been destroyed," and "to set new monuments at such points as may be necessary and be chosen by joint accord."

In keeping with the trend toward consolidating a well-demarcated and enforceable line, the convention agreements stipulated "that the distance between two consecutive monuments shall never exceed 8,000 meters, and that this limit may be reduced on those parts of the line which are inhabited or capable of habitation." In the course of their ensuing work, the commission found that most of the original markers were "but rude piles of stone . . . while the intervals between them were found to be in some cases as great as 20 or 30 miles . . . and in one instance 101 miles." Some monuments had disappeared altogether, spirited away by wind and water or swallowed by the landscape, as if they had never existed at all.

The fulfillment of the commission's duties ultimately led to the repair and replacement of 43 of the original boundary markers and the erection of 215 new iron monuments. The report filed by the commission boasted that the 675 miles of borderline that ran from the Pacific coast to the Rio Grande were now better established and more clearly marked than ever before, with the average distance separating the monuments a mere 2.6 miles. It thus became likely, for the first time in history, that a person crossing north or south at any point along the line would see evidence of a boundary laid out upon the earth, tiny obelisks reaching up toward the vast arc of the sky.

MORALES AND I ARRESTED TWO MEN WALKING AIMLESSLY through the desert night, far from any known trail. The men did not run but fell to their knees, their hands trembling above their heads in the pale glow from our flashlights. They followed our commands, nodding timidly. As we walked them single file to the patrol vehicle, I observed their gait—heavy and sapped of purpose.

Outside the processing center, Morales and I talked with the men while we searched their belongings. They were our age, mid-twenties, and both hailed from the same mountain village in Oaxaca. One of them wore a baseball hat with the image of a marijuana leaf embroidered on the front. You think it's cool to wear a hat with marijuana on it? Morales asked him. The man seemed confused. I didn't know it was a marijuana hat, he said. It's the only kind they were selling. His companion, small and potbellied, listened in, concerned. Is that what marijuana looks like? he asked.

Morales and I rummaged through the men's backpacks, setting aside liquids, perishable foods, and anything that might be used as a weapon. In the bag that belonged to the man with the hat, Morales uncovered a pouch of thickly cut carne seca. The man smiled. I prepared it myself, he said, standing a little straighter. Morales looked longingly at the jerky. Have some, the man offered—no se echa a perder. No thanks, Morales said.

At the bottom of the potbellied man's backpack I discovered a bag of grasshoppers and another filled with small dried fish. The man chuckled. Comida típica de Oaxaca, he said. Try the chapulines, he suggested, pointing at the grasshoppers. I shook some into my palm and glanced at Morales before tossing them into my mouth. The Oaxacans laughed. Not bad, I said. Tastes like salt and lime. The men looked at me eagerly. See if you like the charales, they said, gesturing toward the dried fish. I took one into my mouth, grimacing from the heavy salt. I dared Morales to do the same. Fuck it, Morales said, I'm eating that jerky. For a short time we stood together with the men, laughing and eating, listening to their stories of home.

As Morales prepared to escort them into the processing center, I gathered up the items to be discarded. I was about to toss a small water bottle when the potbellied man whispered that I shouldn't throw it away, that it held mezcal made on his family's ranch. His father had harvested the maguey from the mountains around their village, he told me, and it had been aging for six months. It's at its best right now, he said, take it with you. No se echa a perder.

NEAR THE END OF MY SHIFT, MORTENSON CALLED ME INTO the processing room and asked me to translate for two girls who had just been brought in, nine- and ten-year-old sisters who were picked up with two women at the checkpoint. He told me to ask them basic questions: Where is your mother? In California. Who are the women who brought you here? Friends. Where are you from? Sinaloa. The girls peppered me with nervous questions in return: When could they go home? Where were the women who drove them? Could they call their mother? I tried to explain things to them, but they were too young, too bewildered, too distraught at being surrounded by men in uniform. One of the agents brought the girls a bag of Skittles, but even then they couldn't smile, they couldn't say thank you, they just stood there, looking at the candy with horror.

Once agents placed the girls in a holding cell, I told Mortenson I had to leave. My shift's over, I said. He told me they still needed to interview the women who were picked up with the girls and asked me to stay and translate. I can't help anymore, I told him, I've got to go home. As I drove away from the station I tried not to think of the girls, and my hands began to shake at the wheel. I wanted to call my mother, but it was too late.

SEVERAL HOURS AFTER SUNDOWN, MORALES AND I MET AT A remote trailhead to respond to a sensor hit. We hiked slowly by starlight across stony foothills to the place where a small trail dropped down from a low mountain pass. Morales took his flashlight and crouched to the ground with his hand over the face cap, shining a muted light over a small patch of dirt on the trail. This sign is days old, he whispered. He looked up at the black outline of the mountains. I'll bet whoever set off that sensor is still laid up at the top of the pass.

We decided to wait for the group to come down the trail. We concealed ourselves behind a gnarled mesquite tree, Morales sitting cross-legged and me sprawled out on the desert floor, twisting my body until I found a patch of ground free from rocks. Morales smoothed a swath of earth with his hands and began to trace swirling lines as I gazed upward, transfixed by the Milky Way trailing across the sky like a cloud of glimmering dust. For over an hour the whirring of a nearby cricket and the soft pattering of kangaroo rats were the only sounds we heard. Periodically, I broke the silence to call attention to a shooting star, whispering to Morales to ask if he had seen it. Si vato, lo vi.

After another hour of silence, I reached out to touch Morales's knee. Qué? he replied. How much longer do you want to stay here? I asked. Shit, he said, I don't know. We were silent again. I'll bet you there's scouts in these hills, I finally said. They must have watched us hike in. Morales threw a stick at the patch of dirt in front of him. Maybe the sensor hit was bad, he said. We could hike up the pass. If they're still laid up we can bust the group, and if nobody's there we'll check the sensor for foot sign. I shook my head. If there are scouts, the group is long gone. If there's no scouts and the group is still up there, they'll hear us coming before we get anywhere close. I've been up that trail with Mortenson, I told him. The last quarter mile is steep as hell and covered in loose shale. And if the sensor hit was bad in the first place, I said, well, then it's an even bigger waste of time.

We walked back across the desert toward our vehicles. I paused to look up once more at the moonless night sky, and Morales continued past me. After his footsteps had grown distant, I noticed a tiny point of light drifting slowly across the black dome of the sky. Without moving my head, I called out to Morales. Come back here, I shouted into the night. I could hear him grumbling as he made his way back to where I had stopped. Qué chingados quieres? Look, I said, pointing up at the sky. I don't see anything, he complained. It's a satellite, I said, traveling away from the North Star. Shit, Morales finally said, I see it. Cabrón, I've never seen one of those before. Me neither, I said. We stood enveloped by silence as we stared at the sky, surrounded by figures hidden away in the hills and the mountains, figures gazing up at the very same stars, toward barely discernible satellites barreling through the atmosphere, small bodies tenuously tethered to their orbits at the outermost limits of the earth.

WHEN THE CALL CAME OUT ON THE RADIO, I BRACED MYSELF for the smell. That's the worst part, the senior agents would always say, the smell. During my first week at the station, one of them suggested I carry a small tin of Vicks VapoRub with me wherever I went. If you come upon a dead body, he said, rub that shit under your nose, or else the smell will stay with you for days.

I arrived at the scene in the still-hot hours of the early evening. Hart had already been with the body for thirty minutes. It's fresh, he told me, maybe two hours old. It doesn't smell yet. Hart had been flagged down by two teenagers as he was driving across the reservation. They put rocks in the road, he said, gesturing awkwardly toward the boys. He stood with his hands in his pockets and then asked me if I would talk to them. They keep asking me questions, he said. I can't understand them.

One of the boys was sitting on a rock, looking disoriented. I went over to him and asked how he knew the dead man. Es mi tío, he told me. He stared at his hands as he spoke. How old are you? I asked. Dieciséis. I looked at his friend, standing a few feet away with his hands in his pockets. And you? He looked up from the ground. Diecinueve, he said.

The dead man and the two boys all hailed from the same village in Veracruz and had set out together on the journey north. The nineteen-year-old did most of the talking, telling me that a few hours before the man died, he had taken two Sedalmerck pills, caffeine uppers that border crossers often take for energy, and had washed them down with homemade sugarcane liquor they had brought from Veracruz. A few hours later, he said, the man was staggering around like a drunk, and then he collapsed.

I walked over to the body. Hart had placed a shirt over the dead man's face. I lifted it and looked at him. His eyes were closed and he had long dark hair that already looked like that of a dead man. White foam had bubbled up and collected between his parted lips and his face was covered with small red ants traveling in neat lines toward the moisture. His shirt was pulled up at the sides of his abdomen and I could see where his skin was turning purple with dependent lividity as his blood settled to the ground. With the toe of my boot I gently moved his arm, already stiff with rigor mortis.

The nineteen-year-old told me that the three of them had become separated from their group. Their guide had told them to spread out, to hide in the bushes by the road to wait for the load vehicle. They must have gone too far, he said, because sometime later they heard a car stop and then drive off and after that they couldn't find anyone. Alone at the edge of the road, they walked for several miles in the August heat until the dead man finally lay down to die. The boys waited beside the road to flag down one of the infrequently passing cars, but no one stopped for them. That's why they put the rocks out, they said, to make the cars stop.

The boys asked me what would happen to the dead man, if they could come with the body to the hospital. I told them that they could not, that they had to stay with us, that they would be processed for deportation and that the body would be turned over to the tribal police. They asked if the body would come back to Mexico with them, if they could bring it back to their village. I told them that they could not, that the body would be taken to the county medical examiner, who would try to determine the cause of death. I told the boys they would be taken to the sector headquarters, where they would meet with the Mexican consul, that it was the consul who would make arrangements for the repatriation of the body to Mexico. As I spoke, the man's nephew stared at the ground. Maybe the consul can provide you with some documentation, I suggested, something to take home to your family.

The boys didn't want to leave the body, and even as I explained the procedures to them I began to doubt, given what I knew from my short time on the border, whether they would actually see the consul, whether the consulate would actually arrange for the body to go back to Mexico, whether the boys would even receive a piece of paper to help explain to the dead man's family what had befallen him on the journey north. As I spoke to them, Hart came over and instructed the boys to take off their belts and shoelaces and any watches, necklaces, or other jewelry they might have, and to take from their pockets any lighters, pens, knives, or other sharp objects. I looked at Hart. Transport is coming, he said.

Another agent, junior even to Hart and me, arrived to transport the boys back to the station. He brought a camera to photograph the body and as he took his pictures I noticed the dead man's nephew watching in a sort of trance. I explained to the boy that the pictures were required by the police, that they were needed for the reports we had to file at the station, and he nodded his head as if he had heard and understood nothing, like he just knew it was what he was supposed to do.

Before the boys were loaded into the transport unit, I went to them and told them I was sorry for their loss. It's a hard thing, I said. I told them that if they ever decided to cross again, they must not cross in the summer. It's too hot, I said—to cross in the heat is to risk one's life. I told them never to take the pills the coyotes gave them, because they suck moisture from the body. I told them that many people died there, that in the summer people died every day, year after year, and many more were found hovering at the edge of death. The boys thanked me, I think, and were placed into the transport unit and driven away.

The sun had already begun to set as I left the body, and it cast a warm light on the storm clouds gathering in the south. As I drove toward the storm, the desert and the sky above it grew dark with the setting of the sun and the coming rain. When the first drops hit my windshield I could hear the dispatch operator radio to Hart, who had stayed behind with the body, that the tribal police didn't have any officers available and that he'd have to wait with the dead man a while longer.

Later that night, at the end of our shift, I saw Hart back at the station and asked what had happened with the body. He told me that finally the storm had come and dispatch had told him to just leave the body there because the tribal police wouldn't have an officer to take charge of it until the next day. It's all right, he told me, they have the coordinates. I asked him if it had been strange waiting there in the dark, watching over the body of a dead man. Not really, he said. At least he didn't smell yet.

We stood for a few more minutes talking about the storm and about the human body that lay there in the desert, in the dark and in the rain, and we talked of the animals that might come in the night and of the humidity and the deadly heat that would come with the morning. We talked, and then we went home.

I DREAM IN THE NIGHT THAT I AM GRINDING MY TEETH OUT, spitting the crumbled pieces into my palms and holding them in my cupped hands, searching for someone to show them to, someone who can see what is happening.

THE VARIOUS MEN CALLED UPON TO SURVEY THE NASCENT border between the United States and Mexico in the years following the ratification of the Treaty of Guadalupe Hidalgo could not help but comment on the strangeness of their task and the extreme and unfamiliar nature of the landscape. In places, commission reports remarked upon the "arbitrarily chosen" nature of the boundary line and the "impracticable" nature of their work. Survey members noted that "indeed much of this country, that by those residing at a distance is imagined to be a perfect paradise, is a sterile waste, utterly worthless for any purpose other than to constitute a barrier or natural line of demarcation between two neighboring nations." After the Gadsden Purchase, Lieutenant Nathaniel Michler observed to Commissioner William H. Emory that "imagination cannot picture a more dreary, sterile country . . . The burnt lime-like appearance of the soil is ever before you; the very stones look like the scoriae of a furnace; there is no grass, and but a sickly vegetation, more unpleasant to the sight than the barren earth itself."

More than thirty years after the original survey, subsequent surveyors found that the lands adjacent to the border remained "thinly settled" and noted "the prevalence of thorns in nearly all vegetation; the general absence of fragrance in flowers; the resinous character of the odor of the most common trees and shrubs." Giant cacti were described as "strange, ungainly, helpless-looking objects" with "clumsy arms." In places, the borderlands were "beautiful beyond description," with mountains "rising out of the plains like islands from the sea," but elsewhere the landscape was "a hopeless desert," a place of "loneliness and desolation."

The field party that departed from El Paso in February of 1892 to begin the work of re-surveying and re-marking the boundary was a massive force numbering about sixty, which included several commissioners, engineers, and astronomers, as well as a secretary, a field clerk, a wagon master, a blacksmith, a quartermaster, a carpenter, a medical officer, a recorder, a photographer, a topographer, a draftsman, a levelman, and multiple transitmen, rodmen, targetmen, teamsters, packers, cooks, and other helpers. To carry their supplies, the group traveled with eighty-three mules and fourteen saddle ponies. The expedition was further provided by the U.S. War Department with a military escort of twenty enlisted cavalrymen and a detachment of thirty infantrymen "as a protection against Indians and other marauders."

In the opening days of the expedition "men and animals were new and unseasoned to hardship, but in a few days the majority became accustomed to field life, and the work soon progressed rapidly and satisfactorily." To reaffirm the course of the line, latitude was determined by astronomers and their assistants using the "Talcott method" or through an "exchange of signals by telegraph" over the course of ten nights in which the same stars were observed from distant stations. The men also used chronometers, bull's-eye lanterns, steel tape, a Bessel spheroid, a zenith telescope mounted on brick pier, a sextant mounted on a wooden pier, and a Fauth repeating theodolite "furnished, on the horizontal motions, with axis clamps and tangent screws working against spiral springs."

As the surveying party moved across the boundary, contingents of men were continually convened and reconfigured and sent by rail or caravan to initiate duties along distinct sections of the line. These contingents often worked out of new settlements along the border, and the commission's report noted "the grasping and overreaching action of the United States settlers" and "the kindness and courtesy of the Mexican officials." In some areas, the newly annexed terrain was so remote and unknown as to necessitate the dispatching of reconnaissance parties to secure reliable information "concerning water, roads, and the general topographical features of the country." The surveyors described the landscape as bare and ragged, desolate and rough, punctuated by rocky hills and steep, narrow-ridged mountains of stratified limestone and porphyry, red basalt and igneous rock thrust upward alongside empty craters and extinct volcanos surrounded by broken lava.

As they traversed the farthest-flung corners of the desert, the surveying parties passed the gravesites of travelers who had perished before them. "In a single day's ride," the commissioners reported, "sixty-five of these graves were counted by the roadside, one containing an entire family, whose horses gave out and who, unable to cross the scorching desert on foot, all perished together of thirst. Their bodies were found by some travelers during the following rainy season, and were all buried in one grave, which is covered with a cross of stones." As they cautiously made their way along the infamous Camino del Diablo, their reports noted that "during the few years that this road was much traveled," in the rush to California of the 1850s and 1860s, "over 400 persons were said to have perished of thirst . . . a record probably without a parallel in North America."

The surveyors made it clear that "supplying the working parties with water on the deserts was the problem of the survey, in comparison with which all other obstacles sank into insignificance." The commission's final report revealed that the terrestrial portion of the line, "although having a total length of about 700 miles, crosses but five permanent running streams between the Rio Grande and the Pacific." The report took special care in describing the point where the boundary line gave itself over to the Rio Grande, "a variable stream with turbid waters." The river carried "an immense amount of sediment," it noted, "and as a consequence it is bordered by alluvial bottoms, through which by erosion, it is continually changing its bed." It was as if the surveyors wished to acknowledge how the border, no matter how painstakingly fixed upon the land, could go on to endlessly change its course with the whims of a river.

WALKING TO MY TRUCK AT THE END OF MY SHIFT, I SAW Mortenson standing outside the armory with a group of agents. I went up to greet him and then listened as an agent named Beech told the other men about his time as a prison guard. There was this one guy, Beech said, we couldn't keep the bastard from cutting himself. Swear to god, all he thought about all day was how to slash through his own skin. There was hardly a thing he wouldn't find a way to cut himself with. I'm talking pencils, pieces of plastic, chunks of cardboard, you name it. Shit, even magazines—I came into his cell one day and his forearms were covered in paper cuts and a thousand little blood droplets, and this guy just stared up at me like a fucking deer in the headlights. That's fucked up, muttered Mortenson. Hell, said Beech, that's nothing. This same motherfucker, one day I get called into his cell and he's just sitting there with his crotch all covered in blood. Dude had sliced his cock up with a filed-down plastic spoon, I shit you not. The other agents yelled out and one of them threw an empty can of Monster at Beech's feet. For Christ's sake, one cried, holding his stomach. Beech laughed. Shit, he said, how do you think I felt? You should have heard me call that one in to the nurse.

An older agent named Navarro shook his head and grabbed his gun belt, hoisting it a little higher under his sagging belly. Some people are just like that, he said, les vale madre. A few of the other agents nodded. I was in Iraq with this crazy white kid, Navarro told the group, he had one of those cock piercings. The agents winced. Other guys in the unit were always giving him shit because he was into heavy metal and freaky as hell. We started calling him Marilyn Manson. Mortenson chuckled and Navarro glanced at him. It gets worse, vato. This kid was always looking at these fucked-up magazines, pornos with tattoos and piercings and shit, and one day he shows me a picture of a cock head split right down the middle, like a forked snake's tongue. I shit you not, the kid looked at me with a straight face and told me it was next on his to-do list. The agents burst out into a chorus of groans and the same agent who had thrown the can of Monster called out to Navarro over the jeers. Did he show it to you or what? The other agents laughed. Navarro pulled his belt up again and shook his head. Kid never had a chance, Navarro replied. A week later he got blown up, vato, just like that. I saw it with my own eyes.

The other agents became quiet and several of them looked down at the ground with awkward shame. But Beech remained with his head held up, glancing at Navarro to share a brief nod, as if in acknowledgment.

MORALES WAS THE FIRST TO HEAR HIM, SCREAMING IN THE distance from one of the dirt spider roads. He hiked for a mile or two and found a teenage kid lying on the ground, hysterical. For more than twenty-four hours he had been lost in a vast mesquite thicket twenty miles from the border. The coyote who had left him there told him he was holding back the group. He handed the kid half a liter of water, pointed to some hills in the distance, and directed him to walk toward them until he found a road.

When I arrived the kid was on the ground next to Morales, lurching in the shade and crying like a child. He was fat—his pants hung from his ass and his fly was half open, his zipper broken, his shirt hanging loosely from his shoulders, inside out and torn and soaked in sweat. Morales looked at me and smiled and then turned to the kid. Your water's here, gordo. I kneeled next to him and handed him a gallon jug. He took a sip and began to pant and groan. Drink more, I said, but drink slowly. I can't, he moaned, I'm going to die. No you're not, I told him, you're still sweating.

After the kid drank some water, we helped him up and tried walking him through the thicket toward the road. He lagged and staggered, crying out behind us. Ay oficial, he would moan, no puedo. As we crouched and barged through tangled branches, I slowly became overwhelmed by his panic until finally we broke out of the thicket and spotted the dirt road. You see the trucks, gordo? Can you make it that far? Maybe we should just leave you here, no puedes, verdad?

On the ride back to the station, the kid regained some composure. He told me he was eighteen, that he had planned to go to Oregon to sell heroin, un puño a la vez. I hear you can make a lot of money that way, he said. For several minutes he was silent. You know, he finally told me, I really thought I was going to die in that thicket. I prayed to God that I would get out, I prayed to the Virgin and to all the saints, to every saint I could think of. It's strange, he said, I've never done that before. I've never believed in God.

I FINALLY WENT TO THE HOSPITAL TO SEE MORALES. HE'D been in a motorcycle accident. He hadn't been wearing a helmet, and for a while we had been hearing about his head trauma, that he might not make it. I'd been too afraid to see him during the week he'd spent in a coma, and too afraid, still, to see him during the first days after he came out of it, when he would wake up cursing and pulling his tubes out, when he still didn't recognize anyone.

Walking into his hospital room, I was surprised by how thin he was, how frail he seemed. He had bruises under his deep-set eyes, a feeding tube in his nose, an IV line in his arm, and a huge gash across the left side of his skull where half his hair had been shaved off. Ey vato, he whispered to me. I smiled at him. I like your haircut, I said. He seemed far away, his eyes scanning the room as if searching for some landmark, something to suggest the nature of the place he had come to.

Morales's childhood friend from Douglas was there and told me Morales couldn't see out of his left eye, but the doctors thought the sight would come back eventually. Morales's mother and father were there too, speaking softly to each other in Spanish. A little while after I arrived, Cole and Hart came, still in uniform after finishing their shift. They stood over Morales, and Cole reassured him that soon he'd be back in the field raising hell just like before. I could see a wet glaze in Cole's eyes as he spoke. I excused myself from the room, saying I'd come right back.

Outside I stood in the parking lot, trying to gather my strength. I thought about the tears in Cole's eyes, about Morales's far-off gaze, about his parents huddled in the corner, becoming smaller and smaller as uniformed agents filled the room to hover at their son's bedside. My face became hot and I could feel moisture collecting in my eyes. The glare of the sun grew brighter. The outlines of the surrounding cars and trees grew sharp and began to blur. I closed my eyes and took a deep breath. I would not go back, I decided, I would not let the water gather into tears.

LATE IN THE AFTERNOON I TOOK THE BORDER ROAD OUT TO the lava flow, driving for more than an hour across rocky hills and long valleys. The earth became darker as I neared the flow, devoid of brush and cactus. To the south a pale band of sand dunes underlined the base of a nameless cordillera, shifting at the horizon in shades of purple and dark clay. As I drove slowly over the lava flow, I looked out across black rocks glistening as if wet in the afternoon sun, rocks pockmarked from when the earth had melted and simmered between erupting volcanoes, a molten crust cracking and shifting as it cooled.

DRIVING ALONG A SMALL DIRT ROAD THROUGH THE RESERvation, I was waved down by a man in a passing car. We each pulled over on the side of the road and exited our vehicles to talk. The man was tall with long hair and he stared into the distance as he spoke. He introduced himself as Adam, telling me he lived in a nearby village with his family, a place agents referred to as the vampire village. He told me that strange vehicles had been passing through the village, vehicles he didn't recognize as belonging to any of the residents. It's a small place, he said, only us Indians have any reason to visit. People don't pass through unless they're from there, unless they have family there or something.

Adam's wife stepped out of the car and joined us at the side of the road. She stood close to her husband and kept her hands in her pockets except to sweep back the hair from her face. She began to speak to me slowly, as if measuring her words. This morning, she said, just after Adam left for work, a group of men came to our door. I was alone—it was just me and my son. She gestured at their car and her hand trembled in the air. Their son sat alone in the backseat, playing with a misshapen toy figurine. The boy wore glasses like his father and as I glanced at him I noticed how his body would occasionally seize as if struggling to contain some inner terror. Suddenly the boy began to thrash his head and then he looked out the window at us, his eyes magnified by his thick lenses, his mouth open wide as if shrieking in pain.

The men at the door asked me for water, Adam's wife continued, but they weren't wearing backpacks, they didn't look like normal crossers. How do you mean? I asked. We live twenty miles from the border, she explained, lost migrants pass through all the time. But these men were different, they didn't seem lost. They weren't tired, they weren't afraid, you know? They were wearing camouflage pants and they didn't have backpacks. They always have backpacks.

You know, whenever people come to our door, she continued, we give them water and we call the Border Patrol right away and they always just sit there, waiting to get picked up. They just want out of the desert. But these men got upset when I said I was calling Border Patrol. You better not, they said. Then they demanded food and more water. I didn't feel like I had a choice, so I gave them what they wanted and they took it with them back into the desert.

We've had break-ins before, Adam said, while we were away. They rummage through the house, you know, like they're looking for guns or something. They leave things a mess, but all they ever take is food. And they leave the water running, they always leave the water running.

Adam's wife looked down at her feet and continued her story. Later that morning, she said, I heard these noises from out in the desert, like big branches were being snapped in half or something. It was so loud it woke my boy. A couple hours after that I watched through the window as this minivan drove into town past our house and parked next to the church. It looked like it had broke down— there was smoke coming up from under the hood and everything. Two men got out, a Mexican and an Indian, and they started going through the village from door to door. That's when I called Adam at work.

I told her to lock up the house, Adam said, to put the blinds down and wait for me to get home. We've never seen that van before, you know. It's still parked there, right in front of the church. I looked at Adam and his wife. I'll go take a look at the van and run its records, I finally said. If you give me your number, I'll let you know if I find anything.

Soon after Adam and his wife drove off, I stopped a slow-moving vehicle with three occupants driving north from the village. The driver was Mexican and had a shaved head and a cold look about him. He was covered in tattoos, with two teardrops inked at the corner of his left eye. Next to him, a drunk and toothless man swayed in the passenger seat. I asked the man his name and he told me I could call him Michael Jackson. Everyone in the car burst out laughing. Just kidding, he said, I'm an Indian. Everyone laughed again, even harder.

I asked the woman in the backseat for her ID, and when she reached for her purse I stopped her. There better not be any weapons in there, I said. She looked at me and began to laugh and everyone else laughed too, louder than before, in a way that made me sick. I called in their records and was informed by dispatch that the drunk man had a warrant from the county sheriff for drug smuggling. I told dispatch that the man was a tribal member, and asked for assistance from the tribal police.

Back at the car I asked the drunk man to step outside and I escorted him to my patrol vehicle. There's a warrant for your arrest, I told him. Oh, he said, that's okay. I'm going to handcuff you and place you in the back of my vehicle until we get it sorted out, do you understand? That's okay, he said, swaying. I shut the man in the backseat and watched him double over and begin to weep.

I walked back to the car and asked the driver for consent to search the vehicle. The man glared at me. Listen asshole, I said, you can stare at me all you want, but your buddy's smuggling warrant gives me probable cause to search this vehicle with or without your consent. The man shrugged his shoulders. The car's hers, he said, nodding to the woman in the backseat, I don't give a shit what you do. I ordered the man to step outside for a pat-down and the woman began laughing to herself. The driver stared glassy-eyed into the distance as he spread his legs and leaned with his arms splayed against the vehicle. As I pulled a knife from his pocket, I looked up to see his gaze fixed on the distant dust cloud of an approaching police truck.

The tribal police officer, barely nineteen years old, stood at the edge of the road with the tattooed man and the laughing woman as I searched their vehicle. After the search yielded no results, I walked over to the man and threw him the keys to the car. Be on your way, I told him, Michael Jackson stays with us. The woman shuffled back to the car and the man smirked at me, a glint in his eye. As the car slowly made its way up the road, I asked the tribal officer what would happen to the drunk man. Well sir, he told me, I just got word from my supervisor that his warrant is non-extraditable outside of county jurisdiction. He's lucky you stopped him on the res. I shook my head. The officer shrugged. But since he's drunk as hell I'll take him back to the station until he sobers up or someone comes to get him, whichever comes first.

It was dark when I finally drove down the dirt road that led to the vampire village. The place seemed abandoned and I saw no lights except for a lamp hanging in front of the old adobe church. The minivan that Adam's wife had mentioned was still there, covered in dust and surrounded by foot sign. I called dispatch to run the plates and the VIN, but the records came back clean. Through the heavily tinted windows I could see that the backseats had been removed. The inside was covered in dirt and strewn with burlap twine and empty water jugs. There were two spare tires and an extra car battery and patch kits and cans of Fix-A-Flat scattered across the floor. I followed the vehicle's tire sign through the empty village to the two-track that passed by Adam's house. In the desert beyond the house I saw several places where brush had been run over and tree branches had been broken to make way for the vehicle's passage. At the end of the two-track, the tire sign turned into the open desert and the ground became rocky and hard to cut. I inspected the ground for toe digs and kicked-over rocks with my flashlight and scanned the tangled scrub at the edge of the wash for blackened water jugs and spray-painted bundles. I stopped walking and turned off my light to listen. I knew that the men in camouflage were out in the desert. I knew that they had emptied the broken-down van and brushed their load up in some nearby wash or thicket, that they were waiting for the right time to move it again, to load it into some other disposable stripped-down vehicle. And I knew, finally, that I would not find them.

Before driving back to the station, I called Adam at the number he had given me earlier in the day. He was home and I could hear his son crying in the background. I told him that the van's records had come back clean, that I had followed the two-track south of his home and hadn't found anything. I told him that he should call the station if the men came back to the house or if he heard any more strange sounds coming from the desert. He was silent for a moment and then he thanked me. I could hear the muffled voice of his wife and I knew she was still afraid, and I began to wonder if I was doing them some grave disservice, if I should tell them that I had seen the men from the van, that they were still out there and that the men in camouflage were still out there too, and that they would all come back, that they would forever remember the location of Adam's home, that they would not forget his wife and her suspicion. I wanted to tell him to take his young family and move somewhere new, somewhere far from the border, somewhere where his home would not be at the remote crossroads of drug routes and smuggling corridors. I stared out the windshield as I thought of what to say. Finally, I asked Adam why everyone called his village the vampire village. He thought for several seconds and then said he didn't know. He chuckled at first and then he began to laugh and I laughed too because I wasn't sure what else to do. I laughed and kept the phone to my ear, waiting for him to say something more.

ON MY WAY HOME FROM WORKING THE SWING SHIFT, I SAW A man lurking in the darkness at the corner of my street. It was early in the morning, maybe two or two-thirty, and the man was alone, standing under the streetlight as if he was waiting for someone. My headlights passed over him when I turned onto my street, and I could see that he had a shaved head and tattoos. He didn't look at me, but he watched my truck as I passed, and I was seized by a sickening feeling that I was the one he was waiting for.

I continued past my house and kept going for several blocks before turning down a side street. I kept driving, slowly making my way through the neighborhood, not knowing where to go. After a while I felt foolish and turned around to make my way back home. I drove by the corner where I had seen the man and no one was there, just the empty sidewalk, yellow and broken beneath the streetlight. I made a full circle around the block and still I saw no one, so I pulled into the dirt alleyway behind my house and switched off the headlights as I approached my driveway.

I exited my vehicle quickly, leaving my things inside. I went into my house without turning on the lights and made my way through the rooms, still wearing my uniform and my gun belt. I called the police department on my cell phone, pacing back and forth in my kitchen as I told the dispatcher about the man I had seen standing outside my home. I'm an agent, I said. Oh, the woman replied, we'll send someone right away. I hung up the phone and stood alone in the darkness of my living room, hunched next to a window, peering through the blinds at an empty street.

I DROVE ALONE TO THE FIRING RANGE AT THE EDGE OF town. A cold wind was whipping across the grounds, so I piled rocks at the foot of my target stand to keep it from blowing over. Against the cardboard backing, I stapled a large sheet of paper printed with the gray silhouette of a man, concentric squares descending into his chest. I stood at various distances from the target: three yards, seven yards, fifteen yards, twenty-five yards. I practiced unholstering and firing my service weapon with both hands, with one hand, with my body bladed to the left and to the right, kneeling and from the hip, standing on either side of a barricade.

After completing the course of fire, I shot at a smaller target with my own .22 caliber pistol. As I paused to reload, a yellow bird landed atop the target stand. I waited for it to fly off, but the bird continued hopping across the top. I started to walk downrange to scare it off, and then I stopped. I looked around. The range was empty. It occurred to me then that perhaps I should shoot the bird, that I should prove to myself that I could take a life, even one this small.

I dropped the little bird with one shot. I walked over and picked up its body and in my hands the dead animal seemed weightless. I rubbed its yellow feathers with my fingertip. I began to feel sick and I wondered, for one brief moment, if I was going insane. At the edge of the firing range I dug a small hole beneath a creosote bush and buried the bird there, covering the fresh dirt with a small pile of stones.

AT MIDNIGHT ON CHRISTMAS EVE, JUST BEFORE THE END OF my shift, I heard gunshots ring out in Mexico. I stopped my vehicle at the top of a small hill and stood on the roof to watch the sparkling of fireworks along the southern horizon.

After returning home, I woke my mother, who had come to visit once more for the holiday, her eyes bleary with worry and sleep. We sat together in my empty living room, talking through the night-weary hours of the morning, drinking eggnog and stringing popcorn around an artificial tree. My mother asked about my shift. It was fine, I said. She asked if I was liking the work, if I was learning what I wanted. I knew what she was asking, but I didn't have the energy to think of it, to weigh where I was against what had brought me there. The work isn't really something to like, I told her curtly. There's not a lot of time to sit around and reflect on things. A slow look of resignation came across my mother's face. It's my job, I told her, and I'm trying to get used to it, I'm trying to get good at it. I can figure out what that means later.

You know, my mother said, it's not just your safety I worry about. I know how a person can become lost in a job, how the soul can buckle when placed within a structure. You asked me once how it felt looking back on my career. Well, the Park Service is an institution, an admirable one, but an institution nonetheless. If I'm honest, I can see now that I spent my career slowly losing a sense of purpose even though I was close to the outdoors, close to places I loved. You see, the government took my passion and bent it to its own purpose. I don't want that for you.

I cut her off. I was too exhausted to consider my passion or sense of purpose, too afraid to tell my mother about the dreams of dead bodies and crumbling teeth, about the bird I had buried beneath stones, about my hands shaking at the wheel. Mom—I said—let's open a present.

AFTER DARK, THE SCOPE TRUCK SPOTTED A GROUP OF twenty heading north toward the bombing range. The operator said that they were moving slowly, that it looked like there might be women and children among them. He guided us in and we quickly located their sign and then lost it again across a stretch of hard-packed desert pavement. We split up and combed the hillside, hunting for toe digs and kicked-over rocks. As I looked desperately for sign, I thought of the deadly expanses that stretched between here and the nearest highway, the nearest place that the group might stop for aid. On the walk back to our vehicle I became furious. There were supposed to be twenty of them, they were supposed to be slow, but still I couldn't catch up, I couldn't stay on the sign, I couldn't even get close enough to hear them in the distance, and so now they remained out there in the desert—men, women, and children, entire families invisible and unheard—and I was powerless to help them, powerless to keep them from straying through the night.

II

My mother named me for Saint Francis, San Francisco de Asís, the patron saint of animals. At bedtime, she would read aloud to me from *The Little Flowers of Saint Francis,* a medieval anthology of writings about the saint. She read to me of his sermon to the birds, of the brotherhood of poverty, and of the very first nativity scene, which Saint Francis staged with live animals in a cave above the mountainside village of Greccio. She read to me, too, the story of a fearsome wolf that laid siege to the town of Gubbio, devouring livestock and townsfolk when they strayed into the countryside. It is written that in those days the people of Gubbio "were in great alarm, and used to go about armed, as if going to battle. Through fear of the wolf, they dared not go beyond the city walls."

Saint Francis, who lived in Gubbio at the time, announced to the townsfolk that he would leave the city gates and venture to the lair of the wolf. He made his way into the countryside with a small band of city residents following at some distance to witness his dealings with the animal. As he approached, the beast came running at him with open jaws and the look of murder in its eyes, but Saint Francis made the sign of the cross and the wolf closed its jaws and lay quietly at his feet. "Brother wolf," Francis said, "thou hast done much evil in this land, destroying and killing the creatures of God without his permission; yea, not animals only hast thou destroyed, but thou hast even dared to devour men." The wolf lowered its head as if in recognition. "All men cry out against thee," the saint continued, "all the inhabitants of this city are thy enemies; but I will make peace between them and thee, O brother wolf."

Saint Francis proposed a compact: in exchange for the wolf's promise to cease its killing of livestock and townspeople, the residents of Gubbio would feed the animal every day for the rest of its time on earth. "Thou shalt no longer suffer hunger," he told the wolf, "as it is hunger which has made thee do so much evil." The saint held out his hand and asked if the wolf would pledge to obey the promise. The wolf's reciprocating gesture of accord has been depicted through the centuries in paintings, illustrations, murals, and statues. The animal is depicted as bowing its head in agreement, as placing its paw in the hand of Saint Francis, as standing upon its hind legs and leaning against the saint's chest as if to lick his face.

The dentist introduced a small mirror into my mouth, cocking his head and pushing the tool at different angles against my cheeks. For several minutes he picked and prodded at my teeth, scraping my gum line with a long metallic tool. He glanced up at me. Do you know you're a grinder? he asked. I looked at him. Sorry? You grind your teeth, he said. Did you know? Oh, I said. No, I didn't know. Well, he said, it's getting kind of ugly in there. I looked around, feeling strangely panicked. I had no idea, I said. It's nothing to be alarmed about, he assured me, it's really quite common. But it does seem like something you've started in the last few years—there's nothing in your file about it.

What you do for work? the dentist asked as he grabbed my chart from the countertop. I'm a Border Patrol agent, I told him. Wow, he said, that must be exciting. Where are you stationed—here in Tucson or out in the desert? I thought briefly about how much I should tell him, unsure if he was probing or merely being friendly. Well, I answered, until a few weeks ago I was a field agent. I was stationed a few hours from here, out in the middle of nowhere. But I just took a detail to the sector headquarters here in the city. Low-level intelligence stuff. I see, said the dentist. Is the work stressful? The grinding, you know, it comes with stress. The question surprised me—no one had ever asked me so plainly. I paused to think. It's not stressful,

I said, no. Hmm, the dentist said, seems stressful to me. I thought of my dreams. Well, I confessed, fieldwork could be intense sometimes. But I'll just be doing computer stuff now.

The dentist silently jotted his notes in my file. So why'd you leave the field? he asked. Won't you be bored? I began to feel annoyed with his questions, concerned that I was somehow telegraphing cowardice or insecurity. It's kind of a promotion, I said, it's a chance to learn something new. Another side of the job, you know? The dentist looked at me and shrugged his shoulders. I used to have an office job, he told me, there's only so much you can learn at a computer screen. I rolled my eyes and shook my head. Look, I finally said, I don't know what else to tell you. I thought it would be nice to have a break from the field, to live in the city for a while. All right, all right, he said, holding up his hands. I feel you. I'm just trying to make sure you don't grind your teeth out.

HAYWARD GAVE US OUR ORIENTATION. SIX OF US HAD BEEN detailed to the new intel center from various stations across the sector, most of us with less than five years in. He took us to get new identity badges, showed us how to use the keyless entry system, and gave us a tour of the office. It's like NASA space command in here, he joked. The room was cavernous and without windows, filled with the sound of stale air gusting through floor vents. A multitude of double-monitor computer workstations were situated around a wall of television displays offering an assortment of live camera feeds, real-time maps, and live twenty-four-hour news coverage from the major cable networks.

This is where we keep track of it all, Hayward told us. You all will be responsible for maintaining a detailed shift log around the clock and writing up daily reports for the sector chiefs summarizing the significant happenings around the sector. You'll take phone calls from the stations and keep track of emails. You'll collect and disseminate intelligence reports and safety briefs, log the opening and closing of checkpoints and road blocks, monitor weather events like big storms and fires, and on and on. You get the drift. The main thing is for us to keep track of significant incidents at the station level—agent-involved shootings, dead bodies, big-time dope seizures, arms confiscations, apprehension of known gang and cartel members, things like that. You'll field calls from the station supervisors and note the time of incident, GPS coordinates, and star numbers of the agents involved, and you'll write up a brief narrative regarding each event. The rest is pretty much cake. There'll be plenty of dead time, but there's lots of sector brass moving in and out of here, so look busy, keep your boots polished, your uniform pressed, and mind your sirs and ma'ams.

Outside the building, Hayward leveled with us before giving us an early dismissal. For you boys coming straight from the field, he said, this might seem boring as hell for a while, I know it did to me. He explained that he preferred being in the field, but that his wife wanted them to work their way back to northern Virginia. I'll be honest with you, he said, I'm trying to get the hell out of Tucson

Sector. This is a good opportunity for me as a supervisor—lots of promotion potential. Might even help get me and my wife to D.C. someday and that's why I'm here, plain and simple. But it's a good opportunity for you guys too, a good stepping-stone if you want to get your supe bars or a permanent intel position. And hell, you'll work eight-hour shifts five days a week, and you get to live in the city. And there's air-conditioning, another agent chimed in. That's right, Hayward said, you can't beat the air-conditioning.

EVERY DAY AT SECTOR INTEL AN EMAIL FROM THE DEA CAME through a shared inbox. The email contained photographs and excerpted information from open-source U.S. and Mexican news media relating to the recent cartel activity in both countries. The summaries included photos of human bodies that had been disassembled, their parts scattered, separated, jumbled together and hidden away or put on display as if in accordance with some grim and ancient ritual. Victims' faces were frozen in death, reverberating outward from the computer screen without identity or personal history, severed from the bodies they had inhabited and the human relations that had sustained them.

Each email was presented in bullet-point form, offering little more than place names followed by a brief description of the carnage that occurred there. Acapulco, Guerrero: Two dismembered bodies found cut into twenty-three pieces near entrance to karaoke bar, decapitated heads hanging from velvet ropes, faces peeled off and draped on poles. Nuevo Laredo, Tamaulipas: Four mutilated bodies left on display in heavily trafficked downtown area, accompanying narco message—"This happened to me for being a snitch and a pussy, but I swear, I'll never do it again." Tepic, Nayarit: Two unidentified males executed and posed in front of neighborhood shop, reportedly skinned alive before having hearts torn out. Mexico City: Beheaded male left in truck outside elementary school with body seated at the wheel, head placed on dashboard. Zihuatanejo, Guerrero: Two corpses found discarded near freeway, accompanying narco message—"Here's your trash, please send more."

I DREAM THAT I AM CLENCHING MY JAWS, UNABLE TO STOP, unable to pull them apart. I clench harder and harder until an overwhelming pressure builds. Then, slowly at first, my molars begin to pop and burst.

I dream that a piece of my tooth has chipped off in my mouth. As I hold the jagged shard in my hand, I feel other teeth slowly starting to flake apart. I hold my mouth closed so that I won't lose the pieces, until finally they become too many and I must spit them into my hand, where I look upon them with desperation.

I dream that I am grinding my jaws from side to side, that my teeth are slowly catching and breaking as they are dragged across a decaying surface.

I dream that each time I close my mouth my top teeth become snagged against my bottom teeth. I try to carefully unlock my jaws, to slowly separate them, but the teeth pull and scrape against each other, cracking and crumbling in my mouth.

I dream my molars are falling to pieces, filling my mouth like clumps of hardened dirt.

I dream that I am at the dentist's office clenching my teeth in the lobby, pleading with the receptionist to let me in. She gives me a mouth guard but it doesn't help. Waves of pressure surge through my gums, ripping and cracking at my teeth as if they lie upon a fault line.

I dream that I am not dreaming, that I am truly clenching my teeth until they shatter in my mouth. I am desperate to stop myself, desperate for help. This is real, I think to myself. The other dreams were different—this one is real.

FOR HIS BOOK *AMEXICA: WAR ALONG THE BORDERLINE*, ED Vulliamy conducted extensive interviews with Dr. Hiram Muñoz, chief forensic autopsy expert for the Tijuana homicide department, who has dedicated himself to deciphering the language of drug war killings: "Each different mutilation leaves a clear message. They have become a kind of folk tradition. If the tongue is cut out, it means they talked too much—a snitch, or *chupro*. A man who squealed on the clan has his finger cut off and maybe put in his mouth. . . . If you are castrated . . . you may have slept with or looked at the woman of another man in the business. Severed arms could mean that you stole from your consignment, severed legs that you tried to walk away from the cartel. Decapitation is another thing altogether: it is simply a statement of power, a warning to all, like public executions of old. The difference is that in normal times, the dead were 'disappeared' or dumped in the desert. Now they are executed and displayed for all to see, so that it becomes a war against the people."

MY MOTHER CAME TO TUCSON FOR SEVERAL DAYS TO SEE a cardiologist recommended by a friend. When she told me, I was surprised. What's wrong with your heart? I asked. It's nothing serious, she said, just palpitations. She offered a faint smile. It's like my heart doesn't know what to do with itself now that I'm retired.

After my mother's appointment, we made dinner together and sat in my yard watching the sun set behind lava-capped mountains. At the doctor's office I got to talking with this rancher in the waiting room, my mother told me as we sat down to eat, a man with property all along the border. You wouldn't believe his stories. Oh yeah? I replied. I'll bet I would.

She began to tell me about a local boy the rancher knew, a teenager who showed up at school one day with an expensive new car. Everyone in town thought the boy must have been dealing drugs, but the rancher found out that every day after school he would go to McDonald's and buy bags full of hamburgers. He'd take them to a stash house, or to some hideout spot used by border crossers, and sell them for twice as much as he bought them for. He did this every day, the rancher told her, until finally he had saved up enough money for a new car.

The rancher explained how he used to get calls from men who said they wanted to buy land to ranch on. They would buy up property but they wouldn't ranch it, he said, they knew nothing about ranching. They wanted the land so that they could hunt people along the border. They moved in and welcomed other men to join them, men with assault rifles and night-vision goggles and bullet-proof vests. He told my mother that he hated dealing with these men. He hated them, but he understood them.

The man admitted it was hard to ranch along the border. He had lost count of how many times his home had been broken into. Usually the crossers just took food and water, but sometimes they would take tools and other things they could sell.

The Border Patrol is always too far away, the rancher said, they've never been able to do a thing about it. At this point, my mother said, the man became angry. It's inhumane what the government does, he told her. Border Patrol doesn't stop these people at the line, they let them cross and they chase them on the north side—thirty, forty, fifty miles or more north of the border. They let these people wreak havoc on ranchers' land, they let them die in the desert.

My mother narrowed her eyes and looked at me. Is it true? she asked. I think it's a little more complicated than that, I said. I'd call it an unintended consequence. My mother tilted her head and stared at me unbelievingly. I glared back at her. What do you want me to say? I snapped. That agents are purposely driving people to their deaths? Field agents don't write border policy. We just show up and patrol where we're assigned. My mother shook her head as if my words were those of an apologist or a fanatic. I looked away from her. A line of ants made their way up the leg of my chair. Anyway, I said, I'm not a field agent anymore. My mother reached out and touched my arm. I'm glad you're not in the field. What I want more than anything is for you to be safe. I lifted my gaze and looked at my mother's face. She smiled weakly.

This rancher, my mother began again, he told me about these men he would see every so often on the side of the road, men asking for rides back to Mexico. He said they would feign injury or lie in the middle of the road to get him to stop. Once he stopped, the men would get in the back of his truck and refuse to move, they would pretend not to understand when he told them to get out. He said that the men scared him, that they would glare at him with hostility, that sometimes he even recognized prison tattoos on their faces and arms. My mother shook her head. Listening to him, all I could think about was you working out there in the desert, squaring off against men like that all by yourself. She looked at me. I'm so happy you're not out there anymore, she said. I'm so happy you're safe.

I looked out across the yard. Well, I said, at least you're happy. My mother tilted her head. Oh, she said, you don't like the new position? I shrugged. I don't know. Everyone says it's a good move. And sure, it's smart to go into intel after a few years in the field, to work on putting together the big-picture stuff. But I guess intelligence work just sounded a lot more exciting than it really is. I stared at the silhouette of the volcanic mountains in the distance. It feels like a retreat, I finally said.

THE MIGRANTS WHO SURVIVE THE JOURNEY THROUGH Mexico's interior and evade capture across the U.S. border are often shepherded by their smugglers to "drop houses" in the suburbs of southwestern cities and towns. In Phoenix, a police report reviewed by *Wall Street Journal* reporter Joel Millman in 2009 described the discovery of twenty-two men in the small upstairs bedroom of a rental property on a sparsely populated block of homes. "The subjects I found," wrote the local detective, "were all in their underwear and laying in a line next to each other along the walls and inside the closet." The men "had been jammed in so tightly and so long that the wallboard showed indentations from bare backs pressed against it. Pink walls, decorated with the stickers of Disney characters, were stained with sweat smudges. Down a short hallway was a tiny laundry room labeled 'Office.' There, according to captives' accounts to investigators . . . immigrants were beaten and ordered to produce phone numbers of relatives in the U.S. who were then called and told to wire ransom money."

Millman reported that in Phoenix alone, authorities discovered 194 drop houses in 2007 and 169 in 2008. In 2009, Phoenix officials reported that 68 such houses were raided in the first five months of the year, leading to the discovery of 1,069 undocumented migrants. The proliferation of drop houses like these, Millman wrote, marked "a shift in the people-smuggling business. A couple of decades ago, workers commonly traveled back and forth across the U.S.-Mexico border . . . Now, organized gangs own the people-smuggling trade."

This takeover, according to U.S. and Mexican police, was in part "an unintended consequence of a border crackdown." As border crossings became more difficult, traffickers increased their smuggling fees. In turn, as smuggling became more profitable, it was increasingly consolidated under the regional operations of the drug cartels. Every surge in border enforcement has brought a corresponding increase to the yield potential of each prospective migrant. For smuggling gangs, holding clients for ransom is a simple way of maximizing profit. Matthew Allen, the senior agent in charge of the U.S. Immigration and Customs Enforcement office in Phoenix, put it succinctly to Millman: "The alien becomes a commodity . . . One way you raise the value of that commodity is by threatening [and] terrorizing someone."

HAYWARD ASSIGNED ME THE JOB OF PUTTING TOGETHER A report on a drug trafficking cell active in the southwestern part of the state. For weeks I ceaselessly entered names into databases, collected criminal histories, and analyzed smuggling techniques and crossing patterns. I was able to see each time an individual had been detained or arrested, each time they had been charged with a crime by federal, state, or local authorities. I was able to see each time an individual had entered the country on foot or by car, and if by car, the license plate number and registration information and the names and dates of birth of every other person in the vehicle. I was able to ascertain, through public records, the names of anyone— friend, family, or associates—who had ever shared an address with a given individual. I was able to access marriage licenses and death certificates. I was able to browse through alerts placed by a multitude of law enforcement agencies on any particular individual, home, or vehicle, alerts that notified me if a person was known to be violent or incompliant, if a house had been used to hide drugs or undocumented migrants, or if a vehicle had ever been seized containing arms or narcotics or had ever been referred for secondary inspection by customs officials, Border Patrol agents, or drug-sniffing canines. Using a firearm's serial number, I was able to query whether or not a particular weapon had ever been reported as lost or stolen, whether or not it had ever been present at the scene of a crime. I was able to call up the photographs used on each individual's driver's license or state identification card. I was able to stare at their shadowed faces and gaze into their pixelated eyes.

"BODIES STACKED IN THE MORGUES OF MEXICO'S BORDER cities tell the story of an escalating drug war," Julie Watson wrote in 2009. Reporting for the Associated Press, Watson described how the Ciudad Juárez morgue had been modernized and expanded in the wake of the murders of hundreds of women in the 1990s and early 2000s, and how there were now plans to double its size in the coming year. The morgue had seven doctors, Watson wrote, often working twelve-hour days, seven days a week. In two months' time, more than 460 bodies had arrived for examination. To do their work the doctors drew blood, shaved off pieces of skin, sawed through bone, and extracted fingerprints from headless corpses. Some new hires made it only a few days before quitting. One doctor told Watson he was unable to eat after taking the job. Another said that in order to make it through the day she had to regard the cadavers as medical evidence, not human bodies. Still, the doctors all said, they were glad to have a job in a city where gainful employment was hard to come by.

The families of the dead feared identification and retribution, and so a fifth of the bodies in the morgue remained unclaimed. Some families mustered the strength to come to the morgue only to find themselves unable to take the final step of identifying the deceased, of accepting the physical manifestation of their death. They sorted through the objects that had been recovered from the bodies of their loved ones and gathered into boxes. These are their clothes, the families would acknowledge, these are their belongings. But no, they would say of the bodies, that's not them. It can't be them.

In Tijuana, the director of the city morgue told Watson that his staff couldn't keep up with the pace of the killings. The magnitude overwhelmed the interment infrastructure. "When Tijuana coffin makers fell behind during the December holidays," Watson wrote, "the morgue there crammed 200 bodies into two refrigerators made to hold 80." In cities like Tijuana and Juárez, the cycle of violence was so tightly looped, so unending, that cartel members often raided morgues, reclaiming the bodies of victims, comrades, and leaders. The bodies were ferried from one death-ridden place to another, hovering indefinitely aboveground, endlessly lying in wait for a place to rest in the earth.

ON THE MIDNIGHT SHIFT I TOOK A CALL FROM MY OLD station and immediately recognized the voice on the other end of the line. Cole? I asked. Shit, he said, is that you? Mr. Intel? Already stuck on the graveyard shift, I see. I laughed. Well, Cole began, I'm calling to report a mass-casualty incident. Goddamn, I said. That's right, he continued. While you're sitting on your sweet ass watching TV in that air-conditioned command center, wets are dropping like flies out here. Fuck you, I said. Cole snickered. Just busting your chops. After all, someone's got to give some shit to you hotshots at sector. Can't have you forgetting what it's like for us grunts out here in the field.

Cole went on to tell me that just before dark his training unit had come upon a half-naked man curled up in the fetal position on the desert floor. The man had been drinking his own urine for four days. He was barely able to talk, but Cole was able to ascertain that he had been traveling with his two brothers. Cole asked where they were. Behind me, the man said. Together with one of his trainees, Cole helped the man stagger out to a dirt road where he was evacuated by a helicopter to the nearest city. The man's body absorbed six bags of IV fluid by the time he arrived at the hospital. The doctor said he had never seen such thoroughly decimated kidneys on a man still living.

Cole and his agents had spread out into the descending night to comb the desert for the man's brothers. After an hour of looking, they called for a search and rescue team from sector headquarters. Finally, after several hours, they found the two bodies nearly a mile apart, one of them beneath a gnarled mesquite tree, the other lying faceup and shirtless in a wash beside a hand-dug pit, his belly already swollen wide.

After hanging up, I sat staring at the camera feeds on the massive screen in front of me, imagining all the bodies that I knew were out there, undiscovered under trees and in dry washes, slowly returning to the earth. Hayward walked over to me from the back of the room. What's the matter? he asked, startling me. It's nothing, I said. He hovered over me with his arms crossed, waiting for me to reveal something more. I shrugged. Sometimes I just feel like all the real work is out there. I nodded up at the camera feeds. Hayward stared at the night-vision scenes of the desert. Well, he said, it's a different way of seeing things from in here, that's for sure. He looked down at me. To tell you the truth, he finally said, if you want to understand what's happening out there, it helps to know what it looks like from in here, too. He reached down and smacked me on the back. Now write me up that report. He turned to walk back to his computer.

Two hours later Cole called again. You won't believe this, he said. My trainees just chased down a truckload of dope on our way back to the station. Your bigwig buddies are gonna want to know about this one—the vehicle was loaded with 1,800 pounds. Jesus, I said, that's a ton of dope. It sure is, Cole laughed, see what you're missing? I was quiet for several seconds. Any arrests with the seizure? I asked. C'mon now, he said, you know me better than that. All suspects fled the scene. I sighed. Look, Cole continued, I know you boys at sector love your paperwork, but I'm still trying to get home on time. Well, I told him, that's one hell of an abandoned load. Cole chuckled. It sure is.

I DREAM THAT I AM BACK IN THE DESERT, CUTTING FOR SIGN along a far-off trail. I am working in an expanse of boulders and dry, cracked-open mudflats. Looking out at the landscape I feel free, surrounded with sparse beauty, happy to be close again to the desert. In the distance I hear voices and I arrive at the edge of a large rock where I gaze out over a wash to observe a group of smugglers gathered in a circle, speaking in hushed tones. With no time to wait for backup, I decide to jump the group alone. I bellow to announce my presence, to strike fear into their hearts. I brandish my weapon, holding it in front of my face with both arms outstretched. I yell at them in Spanish to show me their hands, to sit the fuck down, to not even think about running. The men look at me, their faces featureless and unmoving except for cold, vitreous eyes. Using pull-string handcuffs I bind their wrists together to form a long human chain. I line them up in front of me and order them to lead me to their hidden drug load. As we walk in silence I begin to fear that they are leading me into a trap, that they might turn at any minute to attack. With my handheld radio I try contacting other agents for backup, I try calling for a helicopter, but no one answers. I pass with the men through a deepening boulder field, trying to hide my panic, until finally we arrive at a high-walled box canyon piled with trash from cartel scouts and drug mules. In a series of holes that have been bored into the walls, I observe a multitude of black wooden chests stacked atop one another. These are our belongings, the men tell me. I pull the chests from the walls and throw them open, searching for contraband and wrapped bundles, but each and every chest is empty. I look out at the walls of the canyon and find that all beauty has drained from the landscape, that I am surrounded only by the sinister threat of violence, by faceless men and stacks of empty chests. Where are the bundles? I demand of them. Their cloudlike faces blink in the darkness. You've already taken them from us.

I AWOKE FROM THE DEPTHS OF SLEEP TO FIND MY PHONE ringing on the nightstand. Thank god, my mother said as I answered. What is it? I asked. She breathed deeply. I just got off the phone with a friend. They told me an agent had been killed in a shooting and they heard the name Cantú on the news. My heart, I swear to god, I can hardly move. No no, I told her. I'm safe, I'm at home. My mother stuttered and spoke over herself. I knew it couldn't be you, she said, I kept telling them you work at a desk now. Of course, I said, of course. I'm fine. Thank god, my mother repeated. There's another Cantú, I told her, he works with the press. He was probably being interviewed about the shooting—he's a public information officer. Oh, she said, of course. Of course that's it. I sat up in bed. Shit, I finally said. An agent was killed?

I arrived at work to find the intel center teeming with uniformed agents and high-level command staff. Hayward came to me at the door and led me outside. Let me fill you in, he said. We walked to the parking lot and stood shielding our eyes from the sun. I'm assuming you've heard? he asked. Yes sir, I said, just what's in the news. Did you know him? he asked. No sir.

Hayward told me the agent had been deployed with a small tactical unit to monitor smuggling traffic in a canyon south of Tucson. After nightfall, the agents got into a firefight with a group of bandits and one of the men was hit. There was nothing the other agents could do for him, he was dead before EMS arrived. As Hayward spoke I looked down and imagined, briefly, the shattered silence of the canyon, the night sky glinting above the agent as the life drained from his body. The other agents at the scene apprehended four bandits, Hayward told me. One of them is in the hospital with a gunshot wound and the other three are in custody. A fifth bandit, probably our shooter, got away. Listen, Hayward said. There's a shit ton of field agents out there right now, crawling all over the desert. They've deployed National Guard troops, intelligence teams and tactical units from El Paso, and auxiliary agents from stations all across the Tucson Sector. They've even got drones and a goddamn Black Hawk down there.

Here's the deal, Hayward continued—I need you on top of your game. Sector brass is in a frenzy, I've got higher-ups doing the high-speed wobble on every side of this. What can I do? I asked. I need you to get with the other intel agents to put together a target folder on those bandits and write up the best damn report you can. He patted me on the back and began to walk with me toward the door. I want to know everything there is to know about those arrests, he said. I want to know every time they've crossed the border, every time they've been apprehended, I want profiles on every family member and associate you can dig up—name, address, criminal record, whatever you can find. I need to know who's a scumbag and who's just a POW. I cocked my head. A POW, sir? You know, he answered, a plain old wet.

MY COUSIN CALLED TO TELL ME THAT MY GREAT-AUNT Frances had died in her sleep, two weeks after her 102nd birthday. I called my mother. They're having a memorial in San Diego, I told her. Can you go? Not now, she said, not with the way my heart is. Can you? I thought for a moment. Yes, I decided, I'll drive there. Good, she said. You can go for the both of us.

The night before the memorial I drank beers with my cousins in a parking lot while we waited for an order of pizza to take back to the rest of the family. We talked about my great-aunt Frances, about my grandfather, about their brothers and sisters, about their mother and father. Frances was hard-core, one of my cousins said, she drank a shot of Canadian Club and ate a raw jalapeño every day right until the end. She was always going on about how we are related to King Ferdinand, said another cousin, laughing. She chewed out my mom at my own baptism, I chimed in, because my mom announced to everyone that she was proud to be Mexican. Frances pulled her aside after the ceremony. We're Spanish! she scolded her. My cousins and I chuckled. Four hundred years in Mexico, I said, and she still clung to Europe.

Frances's daughter took a long drink from her beer. You know the Pancho Villa story, right? she asked me. No, I said. Her eyes grew wide. Well, you know how our family left Mexico when Frances was a girl? Sure. She raised her eyebrows at me. That was right in the middle of the Mexican Revolution. Your grandpa was just a few years old, even younger than Frances. He was born in 1910, you know, just as war was breaking out. Anyhow, the way Frances told it, Pancho Villa's army was riding through the countryside, making war against the landholders. When the family heard that they were riding through Nuevo León to Monterrey, they hopped a freight train in the middle of the night and headed for the border. Frances said that when the sun came out that morning they could see dead bodies hanging from the passing trees. You're shitting me, I said. Nope, that's the way Frances told it. I thought for a minute. Grandpa never mentioned it, I finally said. Frances's daughter nodded gently. He was just a little boy.

The next day I went with my family to the mausoleum where Frances had been laid to rest. Frances's daughter stood before her mother's nameplate on the wall and spoke of her love and tenacity, of her dogged dedication to family and tradition. When she was done I went up to her. The nameplate, I said, it says Cantú instead of Abrams. That's right, she said, smiling. She requested it in her final weeks. She had no feeling left for her married name.

It's funny, my cousin continued, do you know you're the only one who still carries the family name? Your grandfather had five brothers and sisters but somehow it turned out you're the only one who might pass it on. I smiled. I shouldn't even have it, I said. It's only because my mother never changed her name. That's right, my cousin laughed. Your mother is stubborn, just like Frances. You know, I told her, originally there was a hyphen. What do you mean? she asked. My last name, I said, originally it was Cantú-Simmons, after both my mom and my dad. When I was born my mom still wasn't sure what she wanted to call me. They had talked about Joshua, they had talked about Tyler, so when they had to put a name down for the certificate before leaving the hospital, that's what they put. Joshua Tyler Cantú-Simmons. My cousin roared with laughter. What a gringo name, she said.

It wasn't until a few weeks after my mom got me home that she started calling me Paco, the Spanish nickname for her favorite saint. Soon the other names fell away, and after my parents separated, so did the hyphen.

My cousin smiled. Thank god for Saint Francis, she said, saving you from that terrible name. I nodded. I'd be a different person. She put her arm around my shoulder as we began to walk toward the rest of the group. That's right, she said. A name is everything.

After everyone had paid their respects to Frances, the family walked across the street to an older mausoleum that housed the remains of my grandfather and my great-grandparents. I called my mother to ask if there was anything she wanted me to say to her father. Just talk to him for me, she said.

On the bottom floor, my cousins pointed to the names of our forebears on the ornate walls: Anastasio Cantú Garza and María del Calzado Cantú. Upstairs, we found my grandfather's nameplate at the end of a long hallway, three rows up from the bottom and four places away from an open window looking out over an adjacent graveyard. I was surprised by the bright sunlight streaming through the window, bathing the passageway with warmth. I had been here once before, as a young boy at my grandfather's funeral, and I remembered only the faint image of a wide and dark hallway with souls stuck in the walls.

As I stood by the window, Frances's daughter came up behind me. Do you see that? she said. She pointed over my shoulder. Out there past the trees and the city, those are the hills of Tijuana.

I waited as my cousins paid their respects and made their way back through the hallway and down the stairs. When I was alone, I turned to face my grandfather's name on the wall of the dead. Héctor Luis Cantú. I repeated his name in my mind as I turned to look out the window at the hills of Tijuana. Grandfather, I finally said aloud. You can see Mexico from here.

IN HIS CHRONICLE OF THE MEXICAN REVOLUTION, HISTORIAN Frank McLynn writes of the conflict's slow waning from 1916 to 1917: "After six years of virtually non-stop warfare . . . the country-side was a wasteland of bent and twisted railway tracks, gutted buildings, burned bridges, dynamited factories, carcasses of dead horses or makeshift mass graves for the human fallen. Even in the parched deserts an endless vista of devastation could be descried . . . In the cities and towns indigence and destitution were widespread, and hundreds of cripples, limbless men, mutilated veterans and gravely wounded walking hospital cases thronged the streets." The country's northern plain, he wrote, was a "charnel-house of human corpses."

In Mexico, there is an axiom that the country is bound to suffer through hundred-year cycles of uprising. The war for independence from Spain ignited in 1810, exactly one hundred years before the inception of the bloody revolution against the dictatorship of Porfirio Díaz. Death-toll estimates for the War of Independence range from 400,000 to 600,000. The revolution claimed anywhere from 500,000 to two million. Today, one hundred years later, historians, journalists, and policy makers struggle to approximate a tally for the country's ongoing drug war, a conflict that began ahead of schedule, when president Felipe Calderón declared war on the drug cartels in 2006, just two weeks after taking office in the most closely contested election in Mexican history.

Calderón campaigned on a promise to "clean up the streets," and more than 100,000 murders were officially tallied by the end of his six-year tenure. In an effort to play down the skyrocketing number of drug war deaths, he argued that the vast majority of the dead were linked to the country's drug cartels. At one point, he went so far as to claim that 90 percent of the dead were criminals. However, academics like Molly Molloy, a research librarian and professor at New Mexico State University who studies violence in the borderlands, argue that "when President Calderón or other government spokesmen say that 90 percent of the dead are criminals, it is also the case that fewer than 5 percent of the crimes have been investigated. And by reading the daily accounts of murders . . . one sees that the overwhelming majority of the victims are ordinary people and that most of them are poor: children, teenagers, old people, small-business proprietors who refused to pay extortion demands, mechanics, bus drivers, a woman selling burritos from a cart on the street, a clown juggling at an intersection, boys selling newspapers . . . and dozens of people who have been slaughtered inside drug rehabilitation clinics."

In 2014, the Mexican government released new data officially recognizing an incidence of more than 164,000 homicides since 2007. Researchers such as Molloy are quick to remind the public that such statistics "probably report a minimum number of the deaths

that have occurred." They do not account for the missing and disappeared, estimated at more than 25,000 in 2012. Nor, of course,
do they account for the high rates of kidnapping and extortion.

These numbers also fail to take into account all those who have
died or gone missing crossing the border into the United States, people often fleeing the violence-ridden towns and cities of their birth.
In 2017, Manny Fernandez reported in *The New York Times* that the
Border Patrol had recorded over six thousand deaths in the sixteen
years between 2000 and 2016. In Arizona's Pima County alone, the
remains of more than two thousand migrants were found. The sheriff of another rural county in Texas told Fernandez that "for every
one we find, we're probably missing five." Even as overall crossings
dropped to new lows, the proportion of migrant deaths in the deadliest counties remained constant or even grew. All along the border,
coroners, county medical examiners, and forensic anthropologists
at state universities and nonprofit organizations struggled to identify thousands of remains. "No one deserves to be just a number,"
one forensic expert told Fernandez. "The idea is to figure out who
they are, and give them their name back."

It is difficult, of course, to conceive of such numbers in any tan-
gible and appropriate way. The number of border deaths, just like
the number of drug war homicides, or the numbers that measure
the death toll of the Mexican Revolution or the War of Independence, does little to account for all the ways that violence rips
and ripples through a society, through the lives and minds of its
inhabitants.

ON A SLOW SHIFT AT THE INTEL CENTER I SPENT SEVERAL long hours compulsively navigating dark corners of the Internet, reading of kidnappings and drug massacres, decapitations and dismemberments, bodies discarded in drop houses. On a Mexican news site I read about the discovery of seventy-two bodies in the state of Tamaulipas near the town of San Fernando—fifty-eight men and fourteen women found twisted atop one another, lying blindfolded with bound hands against the wall of a cinderblock barn. The lone survivor of the massacre was an eighteen-year-old Ecuadorian boy who somehow managed to escape the cartel ranch after suffering a gunshot wound to the neck and feigning death underneath the bodies of his companions. In the throes of an unimaginable terror, he fled for ten miles across the arid coastal plains surrounding San Fernando. Finally, he arrived at a military checkpoint where he alerted the soldiers who would subsequently storm the ranch and discover, after the ensuing firefight, the slumped bodies that would later be identified as migrants from Brazil, Ecuador, El Salvador, and Honduras, souls forever waylaid on their passage north through the crumbling Republic of Mexico. As I read the news I hunched above my keyboard with my head in my hands, pulling at my hair with clenched fists. I felt as if the screens were rattling before me, as if the entire room were beginning to roll away, until finally I heard my name. Cantú, Hayward yelled across the floor, snap out of it.

IN AN EXHAUSTIVE STUDY OF NEWS COVERAGE IN MULTIPLE
borderland newspapers, Jane Zavisca, a cultural sociologist at the
University of Arizona, surveyed ten years' worth of reporting to determine the most common metaphors used by journalists writing
about migrant deaths.

Economic metaphors were predominant, characterizing migrant deaths as a "cost," "calculation," or "gamble." Death is a price
that is paid, a toll collected by the desert. Death is the foreseeable
outcome of "cost-benefit analysis, with measurable, calculable risks
and consequences." Death is the ultimate risk in a game of chance,
the unlucky result of a roll of the dice. Metaphors like these, Zavisca
writes, "naturalize death" and "suggest that migrants bear some responsibility for their own deaths."

Violent metaphors were the second-largest category, depicting
death as the vengeful punishment of an angry desert or the casualty
of a war waged along the border. In such discourse, deaths were
blamed on unforgiving weather, on lethal immigration policy, on a
lack of enforcement against an invading army of migrants.

Dehumanizing metaphors constituted Zavisca's third category.
Here, migrants were depicted as animals, something hunted, the
persecuted prey of smugglers, law enforcement agents, and militant
vigilantes. "Lured" to the border by the prospect of well-paying
jobs, migrants engage Border Patrol "trackers" in a "cat-and-mouse
game" with deadly consequences. "A related metaphor," writes

Zavisca, "depicts enforcement agents as humane shepherds tending to a flock." This allusion "reinforces the humanity of the Border Patrol while it dehumanizes migrants by portraying the Border Patrol as 'saviors.'" An associated livestock metaphor, widespread in Mexico, casts migrants as chickens and smugglers as chicken ranchers—pollos at the mercy of their polleros.

Another subcategory of metaphors describes migrants as "dangerous waters threatening the nation . . . a metaphorical home." Enforcement is represented as an effort to stanch the unwieldy flow of migration, the border as a barrier to be plugged and sealed against a rising tide. The corresponding death toll is "a 'surge,' and the bodies are part of a 'flood' of migrants that overwhelm Border Patrol agents and medical examiners." It is here that Zavisca cites the work of Otto Santa Ana, a sociolinguist at the University of California, Los Angeles, who argues that, ontologically, such metaphors dehumanize migrants by representing them as "an undifferentiated mass."

AT THE BEGINNING OF A SWING SHIFT HAYWARD TOLD US HE had been accepted for a command position at the Border Patrol's tactical operations headquarters in El Paso. It's not Virginia, he told us, but it's two states closer. A couple years out there, he said smiling, and I'll be sitting pretty for a position in D.C.

Two weeks later, on his last day at sector intel, Hayward pulled me aside. Have you ever been to El Paso? he asked me. Sure, I said.

My mom used to be a ranger in a park just east of there. Shit, he said, you're practically a native. How would you like to live there?

I pictured the city's glittering lights, recalling how they reached across the border to form a single throbbing metropolis. I recalled, too, news of shootouts and murdered women across the river, the Juárez morgues brimming with bodies. I thought of my mother fallen in the cracked streets, helped to her feet by a man who told us we were in our home.

I'll cut to the chase, Hayward said. The intelligence team out there is looking for agents. They want guys like you: fluent in Spanish, with intel and field experience. You'd be working under me, supporting tactical operations at headquarters, which means you'd get deployed on intel missions all across the southwest border. He watched my face to gauge my reaction. Nothing's a guarantee, he cautioned. I'm not the only one doing the hiring. But I can put in a good word, and you'd have a hell of a good chance. I looked down at the carpet and felt the air gushing up from the floor vents. It's a paid move, he added. And it would get you back in the field.

EARLY IN THE AFTERNOON, SITTING IN BOREDOM BEFORE the dual monitors of my workstation, I looked up to behold the massive image of a prairie falcon in one of the camera feeds at the front of the room. The bird had landed atop a distant surveillance tower somewhere in the rolling grasslands of eastern Arizona and was looking directly into the lens of the camera, as if to peer into the fluorescent airlessness of the office. I stood up from my chair and walked closer to meet the bird's interrogating gaze.

What cowardice has caused you to retreat from the desert? Why not return to the border's smoldering edges, why not inhabit the quiet chaos churning in your mind?

I took several steps toward the screen, as if to reach the bird. I'm afraid to come any closer, I wanted to whisper. I'm afraid the violence will no longer shake me.

HAYWARD GREETED ME AT THE EL PASO HEADQUARTERS dressed in a polo shirt and cargo pants. No uniforms? I asked him. That's right, he said, here we live the good life. I followed him through the parking lot, making note of the various buildings as he pointed them out to me—the armory, the equipment warehouse, the weight room. I followed him up a set of stairs to a modular unit with a massive air conditioner humming outside. He gestured at the adjacent building. That right there is the front office, he said, where all the head honchos are. He lowered his voice. Trust me, he whispered, you never want to end up in there.

I followed Hayward through the door and walked with him toward the back of the building, past a small kitchen and a meeting room lined with topo maps to a small office space where two plainclothes agents sat opposite each other at dual-monitor workstations. This is your new team, he smiled, nodding at the two men as they stood from their chairs. These boys are Chuco Town natives. He pointed first at the older agent, who reached out to shake my hand. This here is Manuel, he told me, he's our expert in scout communications, radio intercepts, signal triangulation, geolocation, all that good stuff. Knows more than I ever will, that's for sure. You can think of him as our team dad. Manuel smiled at me. That's right mijo, soy como tu papá. Hayward gestured at the other man and paused. Beto here, well, I'm still trying to figure out what he's good at. Beto threw up his hands. No seas malo, boss. Hayward laughed. Just kidding, he said. Beto's our equipment guru—he's installing big-ass signal receivers in all our rides, outfitting a travel trailer to be our mobile command center, and he claims to be pimping out our ATVs, whatever that means.

Beto and Manuel smiled and stood staring at me for a few moments before looking back at Hayward. Oh, Hayward said, I almost forgot. He looked at them and placed a hand on my back. Cantú here is still a little green, but he can research the shit out of just about anything, knows how to mine any database you can think of, and can write one hell of a report. Qué bien, Beto said, because yo no hablo mucho English. Hayward rolled his eyes. Very funny, he said. He looked around the room one more time. Am I missing anything? Manuel looked at me and sat back in his chair. Where are you from, mijo? he asked. Arizona, I said. Beto's eyes lit up. Hey güey, did you find a place to live yet? I'm still looking, I said. You married? Got kids? I shook my head. Beto leaned forward and snapped his fingers. Mira, he said, I've got this casita in my backyard I've been trying to rent out, it's like a one-room apartment, perfect for a guy like you. He grabbed a pen and tore a page from a notebook on his desk. Here's my number güey, call me and we'll talk about it. Manuel whistled. Damn Beto, that was fast. All right boys, Hayward said, motioning for me to follow him out of the office, that's enough sweet talk for now.

Hayward walked me back to my car and handed me a stack of documents. I need these filled out by Monday for HR, he said. Show up an hour early and I'll take you over to the warehouse to get you outfitted with some new gear. I took the documents, glancing into the distance at the Franklin Mountains. I'm glad to be here, I told Hayward. Good, he replied, I'm happy to have you. But listen, he said, I need you to hit the ground running. We deploy to Lordsburg, New Mexico, in two weeks for our first mission. I'll be ready, I said.

IN *ANTÍGONA GONZÁLEZ*, MEXICAN POET SARA URIBE RE-imagines the Greek tragedy of Antigone set in modern Mexico. In a translator's note to the English edition of the book, John Pluecker writes that in Sophocles' canonical play, "Antigone could not bear the dictate of Creon to leave her brother's dead body exposed and unburied on a dusty plain. In Uribe's version, Antígona González is bereft of a body to mourn, a body to bury." Pluecker explains that Uribe's book, written as a kind of long-form documentary poem in response to an ongoing plague of disappearance, is actually "one text made out of many," using direct quotations and language lifted from academic and philosophical texts, blog posts, newspaper crime reports, and testimonies gathered by Mexican journalists.

In Uribe's poem, Antígona González searches for the body of her missing brother, and in doing so, inhabits the consciousness of all those who suffer disappearance: "Day after day our certainties have slipped away from us." When grappling with a loss that is incomplete and unending, "there are some who search as a way to refuse to remain in the silence to which they've been relegated. There are some who inquire time and time again as a means to confront their misfortune." In turn, Antígona González imagines the declarations of those who come like pilgrims to sites of massacre, to wherever they may find bodies that remain unidentified and nameless:

I came to San Fernando to search for my brother.
I came to San Fernando to search for my father.
I came to San Fernando to search for my husband.
I came to San Fernando to search for my son.
I came with the others for the bodies of our people.

Antígona González asks: "What thing is the body when someone strips it of a name, a history, a family name? . . . When there is no face or trail or traces or signs . . . What thing is the body when it's lost?"

WE ARRIVED IN LORDSBURG IN THE LATE AFTERNOON AND checked into our hotel. Hayward handed Beto and me a set of key cards and explained that we'd be sharing a room. Budget cuts, he said with a grin. Beto groaned. Hey now, Hayward said, you two are practically roommates, right? He smacked Beto on the back. You already live close enough to watch each other shower across the yard, so this won't be much different. Manuel chuckled as Beto shook his head. That's cold, boss.

At sunset we drove across the railroad tracks to a Mexican restaurant, the only business in a row of abandoned storefronts. Inside we were met with sidelong glances as we sat down in our uniforms near the door. A long silence hung in the air as the waitress handed us our menus. After ordering, we spoke quietly to one another until an older couple stopped at our table on their way to the door. Thank you gentlemen for your service, the man said, nodding at Hayward. His wife smiled. You boys stay safe out there. Thank you, we said.

As we ate our dinner, Manuel pointed to a small boy standing near the door of the restaurant, staring at us with his eyes wide and his mouth agape. His mother hurried over to him and bent down to speak to him in Spanish. Vámonos ya, she whispered, tugging on his arm. But the boy stood transfixed, staring at our guns and the fabric badges sewn to our shirts. His mother looked up apologetically. He wants to be a police officer when he grows up, she explained, pushing her child away from us.

The next morning I awoke early and went to run east along the train tracks toward the rising sun. I could feel my body filling with strength while I ran, swelling with a sense of comfort beneath the wide arc of the sky. Later, riding with Manuel and Beto through the winter-blanched grasslands and playas of New Mexico's boot heel, I felt almost giddy to be back in the field after more than a year behind computer screens. The three of us were silent as we drove, listening to the occasional sounds of our equipment scanning the radio waves for secret frequencies used by cartel scouts. As we neared the line, crackled voices began to filter in through our devices and I pored over topographic maps in the backseat, looking for hilltops and other high places that might provide a vantage point for surveying the terrain and monitoring the comings and goings of marked enforcement vehicles like ours.

Back in the hotel room that night, I was visited by flickering images as I slept. I dreamed of a cave littered with body parts, a landscape devoid of color and light. I saw a wolf circling in the darkness and felt its paws heavy on my chest, its breath hot on my face.

I awoke to Beto's snoring. I fumbled for my notebook in the dim light from my phone, then shut myself in the bathroom and sat on the toilet with the light on and the fan running, hurriedly scrawling every detail I could remember from the dream. Then, for several minutes I stared into the mirror, trying to recognize myself.

IN THE MORNING I ARRIVED LATE TO MEET HAYWARD AND the others at the breakfast tables in the hotel lobby. No one greeted me as I sat down with a bowl of cereal and a cup of peach yogurt. Eventually Manuel looked up from a plate of watery scrambled eggs. Listen mijo, he said, Beto tells me you've been jacking off in the bathroom in the middle of the night. The table went silent and then Beto and Hayward burst into laughter. I looked at Manuel. Shit, I said—I was trying to be quiet. I looked at Beto and bowed my head. I'm sorry man, I said. I just didn't want you to know that I was on the phone with your mom. Beto punched me in the shoulder as the others doubled over laughing. No me chingues, he said. My mom doesn't go for güeritos like you. Hayward leaned back in his chair. Shit, he said, you boys crack me up. He stood from the table and adjusted his gun belt. Beto looked at him. Damn, boss, he said, those are some shiny boots. That's right, Hayward said, I've got more meetings with the brass at Lordsburg station today. You don't think I got to the top by dressing like you, do you? He pushed his chair in. I'll see you boys tonight.

On the drive south toward the border I rested my head against the window, trying to escape the images rattling in my mind, searching for relief in the views of broad valleys and wooded mountains. I found myself inspecting the scenery for signs and clues, for something that might explain the wrenching nature of my dream. I was aware that wolves had once roamed freely through these mountains and valleys, until they were deemed a menace and stamped out. I was aware, too, of the animal's tentative reintroduction to the landscape—small, carefully bred packs released into closely monitored pockets of wilderness to slowly reinhabit a terrain that had once been their own.

I was jarred from my window-gazing by the jangling of Beto's cell phone. I can't hear you, ma, I heard him say, tranquila. He turned to Manuel and asked if he would pull over. After the vehicle came to a stop, he opened the passenger door and wandered into the grass at the side of the road, pressing the phone to his ear. I watched as he paced back and forth and then finally put the phone in his pocket to stare at the grass bending at his knees.

We continued south across the Animas Valley on a broad dirt road. Suddenly Manuel slowed to a stop. What is it? I asked. Shhhh, Beto whispered, pointing to the road. There, barely five yards from our sputtering vehicle, an antelope stood staring at us through the windshield, regarding us with wide, shining eyes, as if we were a band of misfit ghosts. Outside the passenger window, another animal shuddered beside the road, too fearful to follow its partner. Later, as we drove up into the pine-oak woodlands of the Peloncillo Mountains, a pack of coatimundi, thirty strong, paid us no mind as they swarmed the road in front of us, sniffing the dirt with pointed noses, their round bellies low to the ground, their tails held high in the air.

We stopped at an abandoned campsite deep in the Peloncillos to eat our bagged lunches. Beto and I sat across from each other at a picnic table while Manuel stayed in the vehicle to listen to the scanner. Is everything all right? I asked Beto. He set his sandwich on the table. It's my cousin, he said. He died yesterday in Juárez. My mom just got the news. She doesn't yet know how it happened. We ate our sandwiches in silence, then Beto laughed to himself and began to tell me stories. He told me about crossing the border with his cousin to party in Juárez when they were still too young to drink. He told me about house parties in El Paso, about drinking in the desert at the edge of town, about the two of them chasing girls at the clubs and bars when they finally turned twenty-one. He trailed off and shook his head, and I watched his eyes track the movements of a red bird fluttering between the branches of an oak tree. It's weird, Beto said, all these animals. He paused, thinking. You know, yesterday when I was pissing at the edge of the road, a black butterfly flew right in front of me—a big one. I can't stop thinking about it. He continued nervously, as if he was afraid of what I might think. A few years back, the day before my grandma died, I saw one just like it in the West Texas desert, flying out across the grass.

AT NIGHT, OFF DUTY, HAYWARD DROVE US UP INTO THE mountains. As we climbed, we could make out white patches of snow on the sides of the highway. We drove into town, parked by the old theater, and walked straight to the nearest bar, a place called the Buffalo. After we'd ordered, I put a handful of quarters in the jukebox. When the first notes of Marty Robbins's "El Paso" began to ring out, Beto smiled widely and looked over at me, letting out a Mexican grito.

After our first beer, I walked with Manuel through the cold to a nearby gas station to buy cigarettes. On our way back we stopped at a bridge over a deep-set creek and blew smoke as we spoke into the dark air. My wife and I are going to buy a house, he told me, on the east side of El Paso. That's great, I told him. Congratulations. Manuel stared down into the creek. No one in my family's ever owned a house, he said.

Back at the bar Beto was talking with a middle-aged woman, his hand resting on her thigh. This is Suzy, he smiled. She says we ought to go up the mountain to the opera house. Shit, said Hayward, that sounds fantastic. We left the bar and crowded into his truck with Suzy in the front seat guiding us up a winding road. The windows of the old opera house glowed with warm light and inside it teemed with people and smelled of wood smoke. The floors and the ceiling were made from wood and the adobe walls looked the same as they might have a century ago. We sat and ordered beers and listened to the men singing and playing fiddle, our bodies absorbing the warmth and the smoke and the sound of it all. Outside I stood with Hayward to escape the crowd and he told me about his wife, about how he married his best friend, how you know you've met the right person when they don't aim to change you but appreciate you for who you are.

Manuel and Beto tired quickly of the fiddle music and soon we were driving back down the mountain with Suzy to have one last drink at the Buffalo. After another round of beers Beto began to sway. He danced with Suzy, putting dollar after dollar into the jukebox. Hayward, still sober, sat with Manuel and me, telling us about growing up in Virginia. He was a quarterback in high school, he told us, and his wife was the head cheerleader. That's how we first met, he said, at the football games. Hayward's father, a police chief, encouraged him to join the force as soon as he graduated from high school. Hayward was the youngest recruit they'd ever had.

An old country gospel song came on and Hayward smiled. Before all that, he said, I used to sing in a gospel group with my brothers and sisters. We toured around some, he said, opened for some pretty big shows. He smiled. One of our songs got recorded by one of the big gospel acts. I turned away and saw Beto leaning in to kiss Suzy.

As Hayward drove us back down the mountain, Beto snored in the passenger seat while I stared at the lights of the town in the valley below, twinkling like a place of happiness and promise.

I DROVE WITH MANUEL AND BETO THROUGH A BROAD DESERT valley to the border. For several hours we sat parked next to a water tank in a low canyon, listening on the radio scanners to the scouts, one on a hilltop to the west and another in the mountains above us. A man with the code name Metro 4 called to Alpha 3, describing our every move along the dirt road, noting each time we turned or parked or stepped out of the vehicle to piss. The scouts left their positions at nightfall and the frequencies went silent.

The next day when we resumed our sweeps the frequencies were still quiet. At night we parked at the water tank and the stars glared above us in a moonless sky. We sat in our vehicle and listened to a cartel lookout crew south of the line. Manuel told us that they were following an armed convoy along a Mexican highway. We could hear how the men worked themselves into a frenzy, how some of their voices cracked with the excitement and adrenaline surging through their bodies and how others whimpered with panic. The lookout crew is in charge of protecting the local boss, Manuel explained, and the convoy is made up of members of a rival cartel. Later, a man named Víctor Chulo came on the radio and told his crew that the convoy was passing through the territory with the blessing of the boss. They're probably on their way to a cartel ranch for a high-level meeting, Manuel told us. I imagined what the ranch might be like, how the stars might look from there. It must be up in the mountains, I thought to myself, hidden in a beautiful place where I must never go.

BEGINNING IN 2008, THE WRITER CHARLES BOWDEN CON-ducted a series of interviews with a former cartel hit man, known in Mexico as a sicario. Bowden eventually arranged for the sicario to sit down for several days of videotaped interviews with Molly Molloy and the Italian filmmaker Gianfranco Rosi, who compiled his testimony in the documentary *El Sicario, Room 164*. As a condition for appearing on film, the sicario insisted that his voice be altered and his face obscured, so it was agreed, at Rosi's suggestion, that he would wear a black veil over his head, much like the hoods used by executioners of old.

In Bowden's preface to the book that compiles these interviews, he writes of the sicario: "Nothing in his appearance signals what he has been and what he has done." Yet he has managed "to kidnap people, torture them, kill them, cut them up, and bury them when the rest of us cannot imagine doing such things." In his testimony, the sicario describes the act of killing: "I never doubted at the moment I got the order, I never doubted, I just pulled the trigger. I could not even think. I did not know the person . . . For me, it was nobody."

He goes on to explain how, almost as a rule, he and all the cartel men he knew and worked with were always high and drunk when carrying out their work. After killing or torturing a target, the sicario says, "I did not fully realize what I had done until two or three days later when I was finally sober. I realized how easy it was that the drugs and the world that I was in were controlling and manipulating me. I was no longer myself."

When those they had kidnapped were executed, the bodies were buried in mass graves known as narcofosas. "I think that here in the border region that . . . well, let's say that if there are one hundred of these narcofosas, maybe only five or six of these places have been discovered," the sicario says. "I cannot tell you exactly how many people have been buried in this fashion. It is impossible to say." Nevertheless, "these numbers are very important, very representative.

One hundred persons. Can you imagine one hundred people buried in a cemetery, but they are piled one on top of another? Can you imagine trying to identify, trying to recognize those people? Can you imagine in a one-hundred-twenty-square-meter lot . . . that there are fifty people buried in a common grave?" The sicario describes the lengths to which the cartel goes to obscure the identities of its victims: "It is necessary to put lime and other chemicals on the bodies," to "remove all of their clothing and other belongings so that the bodies will not leave any traces, so that they cannot be located or identified."

AFTER OUR TEAM CONCLUDED ITS OPERATION IN NEW MEXico, my coworkers returned to El Paso for the weekend and I stayed behind to pay a visit to my uncle, who had recently retired and moved from Santa Fe to the outskirts of a small town in the boot heel. I arrived Friday night after dark and my uncle greeted me at the door, hunched and backlit by the warm glow from the house. He hugged me under the porch light. It's been years, he said. He backed away to inspect me, his hands at my shoulders. You look strong, he said, gesturing for me to come indoors.

Inside, the house was filled with boxes and unarranged furniture. He let out a nervous chuckle. I'm just renting until I can get something built out at the property. His eyes gleamed. We'll go out for a hike tomorrow, he said, and I'll take you by the site. You can tell me what you think.

In the morning I awoke on the couch and found my uncle gone. I browsed lazily through the living room, looking through boxes of my uncle's old photographs. There were images of him and my father, his only brother, hiking through the mountains of Southern California and New Mexico, grinning as they tied fishing flies onto long lengths of line and arched their rods toward sparkling streams. My uncle, having no children of his own, had collected endless images of me and my half siblings—each of us separated from the other by many years and great distances. There were pictures of us as infants, as toddlers, as young children posing clumsily for our elementary- and middle-school photographs. Farther down in one of the boxes were images of my father beaming at the side of our young mothers, his many past wives. In one photograph, he stands at the edge of the sea with the mother of my youngest half sister. In another, he stands on a green hillside with my mother on the first day of their short marriage, my mother luminous in a white cotton blouse and a purple shawl, my father with a striped shirt loose and whipping in the wind.

I looked up from the box and glanced out the window to see my uncle making his way toward the house. I stood and watched him from the kitchen window as he jogged down the dirt road in a slow and gangling manner, his hands sheathed in leather work gloves. For years a degenerative disease of the peripheral nerves had been coursing through his body, eating away at the muscle tissue in his feet, arms, and hands. Unable to flex his calves to draw up his forefeet, he lifted his knees all the way to his waist in order to run without stumbling. The gloves, he told me later, were to protect his hands when, inevitably, he tripped and fell to the ground.

After a small breakfast my uncle took me out to the property along the Arizona state line where he had laid the foundation for his new home. It's not much, he said, shrugging. I looked out across his flat and dry acres, laid over with pale grass and tangled thickets of mesquite. I could sense that he held misgivings about the isolation, that he was eager for me to find something of worth in the yawning landscape, the tremendous dome of clear sky. I'm not sure exactly what it is, he said as he looked out at the property with his hands on his hips—I guess it just feels good to be close to a place that's still wild. I looked across his land to the horizon. You can see mountains in every direction, I said.

We drove west toward a trailhead at the base of the Chiricahua Mountains and stopped at the place where a creek, cold with snow-melt, flowed over the dirt road. My uncle ushered me out of the car and pointed to the pale and leafless trees looming at the banks of the creek. I came here for the sycamores, he told me. He lifted his legs to step over the rocks at the edge of the creek, explaining how the trees reminded him of the sycamore canyons that cut through the mountains of Southern California, where he'd spent his young summers working in an apple orchard with my father. He told me about the day he first came to this spot, on honeymoon with his second wife in 1992. He recalled how they stumbled upon this same creek bed flowing across the road, and then, as if recounting the discovery of some cherished thing long ago traded away, he described his breathless surprise at finding these great white trees from his youth. I couldn't sleep that night, he said, because of the sycamores. The next day he and his wife went driving in the mountains above the creek and came across a small and perfect apple orchard. My uncle looked upstream. I've been back up in these mountains time and again since I moved here, he told me, but I can't find a trace of it. Not even an overgrown clearing, not even an old stump. He rubbed his hands against the cold and stared down at the slow current of the creek. I still dream of apple orchards, he said, twisting his face at the water.

We arrived at the trailhead in the late morning and set out together up the north fork of Horseshoe Canyon. As we hiked past fire-blackened trees, my uncle began to recount all the natural things he had been made to destroy in the years he worked as a contractor in Santa Fe. At one job site he tore down a mighty pine tree and cut it into pieces. On another job he carved a road into a still-wild hillside. He described the guilt that consumed him in the weeks after such acts, visiting him even in his sleep. It's overwhelming sometimes, he said, to think of all the trees I've killed, all the scars I've left in the land.

I wanted to tell my uncle that I had known men to do much worse, that I still carried with me images of landscapes laid to waste, places riddled with the shells of burnt-out vehicles and piles of rusting bicycles, places where even the most isolated trails and roads were lined with every kind of trash imaginable—blankets and burlap bundles, old clothes and cut wire, twine and pull-string handcuffs and gallon water jugs painted black, stomped and slashed open, awaiting the slow decay of coming centuries. I wanted to tell my uncle that I had known men to engage in senseless acts of defilement, depositing car seats and furniture on far-off hilltops and in remote washes, decorating cacti with women's undergarments, hanging twisted bike frames from the towering arms of saguaros, dislodging massive boulders to tumble down sloping mountainsides, and setting fire to anything that would burn—abandoned automobiles and trash piles and proud desert plants left to smoke and smolder through the night.

We continued hiking until we arrived at the high wall of a crumbling dam, where we decided to stop for a lunch of apples, cheese, and peanut butter. As he ate, my uncle seemed to me like a small and gentle bird, and I wondered at his capacity to demolish the landscape, despite his need for solace in wild places. He turned to me and smiled. How's your job? he asked. I chewed an apple, thinking of how to reply. I wanted to tell him that I had reached a point at which I could barely sleep, a point at which my mind had become so filled with violence that I could barely perceive beauty in the landscape around me. I wanted to tell him that I feared there was nothing for him here, that he would find no peace in these borderland deserts. I breathed a deep breath and looked over at the water held back by the sagging dam. The job is good, I finally said. It's nice to be out of the office, to have some work back in the field. My uncle leaned on one arm and joined me in looking out across the dark waters of the lake.

Later, as we made our way back to his truck, I thought briefly that I might tell him about the wolf dream, that I might confide in him my fear of coming unraveled. We walked side by side and I watched as he lifted his knees, his dangling feet thudding upon the trail. I worried, briefly, that the blood that ran in him might be the same that runs in me. Blood that fills the head with visions, that pulses away at sleep, that eats slowly at the muscles. Blood run through with ruin.

I JOGGED THROUGH THE STREETS OF EL PASO TO RIM ROAD and up Scenic Drive. The air was cold and thick after a winter rain, and white wisps rose from the smokestacks east of the city. To the south I looked across an expanse of streets and buildings to where dark clouds had gathered over the tops of the Juárez Mountains, above white words that had been built into the mountainside with massive piles of painted rock: "CD JUÁREZ," they read. "LA BIBLIA ES LA VERDAD, LEELA." The lettering was ugly and crude, but it reminded me where I was, above two cities stretching across the floor of a once mighty river basin ringed by arid and stony peaks, seething and glimmering as their residents prepared for the coming night.

To live in the city of El Paso in those days was to hover at the edge of a crushing cruelty, to safely fill the lungs with air steeped in horror. As I ran and drove through the city, oscillating from work to home, the insecurity in Juárez drifted through the air like the memory of a shattering dream. In news, in academic texts, in literature and art, the city was perpetually presented as a landscape of maquiladoras, narcos, sicarios, delinquents, military, police, poverty, femicide, rape, kidnapping, disappearance, homicide, massacres, shootings, turf wars, mass graves, corruption, decay, and erosion—a laboratory of social and economic horror. This narrative, of a city fractured by its looming border, saddled with broken institutions and a terrorized populace, had become part and parcel of its legacy, the subconscious inheritance of all those who came within the city's orbit. To comfortably exist at its periphery, I found myself suspending knowledge and concern about what happened there, just as one sets aside images from a nightmare in order to move steadily through a new day.

Now, as night settled over the valley, I struggled to discern the exact location of the border as it flowed through an illuminated expanse. I thought about the places I had seen in Juárez: the turnstiles and taco stands, the storefronts and snack vendors, the blinking stoplights and the intersections teeming with cars and people— people I had seen extend, without hesitation, the most basic kindness toward one another, people who lived and breathed in the city as if it were entirely ordinary, as if it were a place worth coming to, worth living in, worth remaining. I held Juárez in my mind and I felt a pull to go there, to walk confidently through its parks, its sidewalks, its market halls. I felt the city's pull even as I knew, with sinking certainty, that I would not go, that something I had chosen now kept me from crossing over.

IN *RINGSIDE SEAT TO A REVOLUTION*, AUTHOR DAVID DORADO Romo examines how the Mexican Revolution "was photographed, filmed, and commodified" from the twin cities on the banks of the Rio Grande, which together served as the "intellectual crucible" of the insurgency. A carnival atmosphere prevailed in El Paso during the buildup to the Battle of Juárez, and both cities were awash with international journalists, photographers, and filmmakers, as well as all manner of mercenaries, thrill seekers, adventurers, and spectators. Tourists from El Paso crossed the Rio Grande to pose with insurgents and their horses in the encampments on the river's southern bank, feigning steely resolve with rifles clutched in their hands and bandoliers slung across their chests.

When large-scale fighting finally erupted in May of 1911 between federal soldiers loyal to President Porfirio Díaz and the renegade armies of Francisco Madero commanded by Colonel Pancho Villa and General Pascual Orozco, El Pasoans "scurried to the tops of trains and buildings" to witness the bloodshed. Twenty-five cents could buy you a viewing spot from the rooftops of the Mills Building, the Sheldon Hotel, the Union Depot tower, or the El Paso Laundry building, and if fighting did not materialize you could ask for your money back. Newspapers in El Paso ran advertisements suggesting, "It is foolish to expose yourself to any danger in connection with the troubles in our sister republic. You can see everything, even to the smallest details, if you get a good pair of field glasses." The urge to witness the mayhem was so strong that "people were willing to risk their lives to be spectators," and during the battle "five El Pasoans were killed and [eighteen] wounded on the American side of the line."

The newspapers reported that Juárez looked "as if a hurricane had struck it." Buildings were blown apart and left to burn through the night. Daylight revealed streets "littered with splinters of wood, plaster, broken window glass and adobe debris." To some, the ruin of Juárez was a thing of wonder. Joseph Sweeney, a former mayor of El Paso, remarked that "it was a beautiful sight to see the shrapnel bursting up in the air and scattering its death-dealing missiles on the hills and in the valleys surrounding." In the aftermath of the fighting, sightseeing cars ran advertisements for trips to the ruins of the "battle scarred city."

Only a year before, the residents of both cities had been brought to their rooftops to witness a very different event—the passage of Halley's Comet across the night sky, visible to the naked eye for more than a month. Seven hundred miles away in Nuevo León, in the city of Monterrey, my unborn grandfather swelled in the belly of his mother. I imagine how his family might have gathered together at some high point in the cool air of an early-summer night, my great-grandparents holding their children close as they gazed awestruck at the cosmos. I imagine tiny Frances, my great-aunt, beholding the comet as an incomprehensible streak of light.

BETO INVITED ME TO GO WITH HIM AND HIS FRIENDS TO A nightclub in downtown El Paso. We made our way through hot crowds of scantily clad women and sweating men, taking turns buying rounds. I watched a woman in a red dress dancing with a man in the roped-off VIP section at the center of the dance floor. Beto leaned toward me and shouted in my ear. I wouldn't look at her if I were you. What? I asked. She's with a narco, he said, lowering his voice. Beto gestured at the man and I watched as he grabbed the woman's hips, his bleary eyes rolling back in his head.

For much of the night I danced with a thin, dark-haired woman. She led me by the hand to an outdoor terrace and I stood in the cold with her as she leaned against the brick wall of the nightclub, smoking a cigarette. I don't like it here, she told me. What do you mean? I asked. Earlier, she said, when I went to use the bathroom, a couple came up to me. They were older, in their forties maybe, they looked like they had money—they were good-looking, you know, dressed in expensive clothes. They spoke Spanish like they were from Spain and they tried to convince me to go somewhere with them, to their house or the house of someone they knew, I'm not sure. There was just something about it, she said, I didn't like it. She hurriedly smoked her cigarette and tugged down at the hem of her dress, then crossed her arms in front of her chest.

Inside the woman drifted away from me and disappeared into the throng. At the end of the night, as the bars closed and young people flooded into the streets and parking lots, I searched for her outside the nightclub, craning my neck to look over the crowds.

BEGINNING IN THE MID-1990S, FEMICIDE—THE KILLING OF women—became the hallmark of Ciudad Juárez, an emblem of the danger and chaos unfurling along the border. Mexico City journalist Sergio González Rodríguez was one of the first reporters from outside the state of Chihuahua to cover the murders for a national audience. In *The Femicide Machine*, González describes the archetypal crime of the era: "The victims were abducted from the streets of Ciudad Juárez and taken by force into safe houses where they were raped, tortured, and murdered at stag parties or orgies. The victims' bodies were dumped into the desert like garbage, tossed onto streets, on corners and vacant lots in the city's urban and suburban zones, and in the outskirts of the city." By dumping their victims in empty lots and trash heaps, González asserts, the perpetrators of these crimes negated the essential humanity of their victims: "To leave a raped, abused, half-naked woman's body in a garbage dump is to resignify the body with indifference and abjection. The act suppresses the distance between objects and humans, and calls out for savage disorder . . . Through it, the victim is reminded of her restricted status in domestic and industrial spheres . . . Her identity is predestined not to exist."

Even as international attention began to focus on the city's femicide, the identities of its victims were obscured by sensational narratives. Women were represented as young and powerless, engaged in exploitative employment in U.S.-owned manufacturing facilities known as maquiladoras, and preyed upon as they bused home from work or reveled in the city's nightclubs. In an interview with *The Texas Observer*, Molly Molloy describes how these narratives served to fetishize victims, representing their bodies as a "kind of sacrificial host" or a "symbol for suffering." She conveys how the sexualized rhetoric surrounding femicide eroticized its targets, making the women, many of whom "do the work and are the only breadwinner," appear more helpless and powerless than they actually were.

At first, the women murdered in Juárez were assumed to be victims of a serial killer. After the suspected killer was caught, subsequent crimes were blamed on alleged copycat murderers or sex-obsessed misogynist gangs. It was implied by local and state officials that many of the women shared the blame for their victimization because of their penchant for frequenting bars and nightclubs. The city was presented as a battleground, an active crime scene. In such places, where the threat of death is incessant, there is little space for grieving. In Juárez, this paved the way for an almost ritual negation of individual loss by both those who sought to bring attention to the crimes and those who sought to dismiss them.

Law enforcement exhibited no inclination to seriously investigate the murders. In 2003, the United Nations Committee on the Elimination of Discrimination against Women visited Juárez to evaluate gender-based discrimination and violence in the city. Its subsequent report found that "thus far, in the cases involving sex crimes, the murderers have acted with full impunity. Nearly all sources, including statements and comments made to the experts by Federal Government officials, the heads of federal agencies and several senators, have made it clear that the local authorities, both state and municipal, are assumed to have a years-long history of complicity and fabrication of cases against the alleged perpetrators."

Sandra Rodríguez Nieto, a longtime investigative reporter for the newspaper *El Diario de Juárez*, writes about interviewing victims of Juárez violence in *La fábrica del crimen* (translated into English as *The Story of Vicente, Who Murdered His Mother, His Father, and His Sister*): "Nearly everybody I've met who has come in contact with the Chihuahua criminal system over the femicide cases has described it as the worst experience of their lives: the victims don't get justice, the defendants lack basic guarantees of safety or legal proofs against them—which makes it highly probable that the actual killers remain at large."

In 2004, the internationally regarded Argentine Forensic Anthropology Team—a nongovernmental human rights organization of forensic scientists established in 1984 to investigate the thousands of unsolved disappearances during Argentina's "Dirty War"—began its own investigation of the Juárez femicide cases. In later reports, the team documented a willfully inept justice system with investigatory bodies prone to "grave methodological and diagnostic irregularities" in identifying female remains. In investigating the more than thirty unidentified bodies taken from mass graves, the team found that state authorities had often failed to label the remains, leading, in some cases, to the mixing together of the recovered body parts of distinct persons, a literal amalgamation of individual victims into an undifferentiated mass.

The unsolved murders in many ways provided a blueprint for the structural underpinnings of the large-scale violence that would soon come to eclipse them. By 2008, little more than a year after Calderón declared war on the cartels, Ciudad Juárez had become ground zero for the conflict. As cartel violence exploded south of the border, Juárez underwent a grim transformation. It was no longer the city where women died, it was the city where everyone died. At the height of violence in 2010, according to *El Diario de Juárez*, more than three thousand murders were reported—an average of eight per day—earning Juárez the nickname Murder City and the dubious title of "murder capital of the world." During these same years, El Paso was named the safest city in the United States.

The indiscriminate killing in Juárez and all across Mexico was so rampant that in 2012, when *New York Times* foreign correspondent Damien Cave reported on a new wave of killings and disappearances among the women of Juárez, even larger than those of the 1990s and early 2000s, attention could not be roused. "People haven't reacted with the same force as before," a human rights investigator for the state of Chihuahua told Cave. "They think it's natural."

MANUEL ASKED BETO AND ME IF WE WOULD HELP HIM MOVE into his new house over the weekend. Beto and I drove together to his home on a Saturday morning and joined his family in unloading a massive moving truck parked in his driveway. His wife directed us as we carried furniture into the rooms and up the stairs. As we lumbered through the living room with boxes, Manuel's two girls ran in circles around our legs. When the truck was finally empty, we sat on stools around the kitchen counter and ate pizza with his family. Manuel introduced us to his mother and father. Este es mi otro hijo, he told them, gesturing at me. I chuckled and reached out to shake their hands. Mucho gusto, I told them. Manuel's father smiled. You speak good Spanish, he told me, are you Mexican? I thought about how to answer. Partly, I said, yes. My grandfather's family came from Monterrey. Ah, Manuel's father said. Soy de Delicias, estado de Chihuahua. But I've been to Monterrey, he told me proudly, I used to drive big rigs all along the border. He sat tall in his stool. Fui trocadero, he said. Conozco todos partes.

Manuel's mother and father began to tell me about the towns of West Texas and the nearby villages of northern Chihuahua and Coahuila. We used to cross the border like it was nothing, his mother said. Manuel's father shook his head. When I retired from truck driving, we took the children and drove all along the border, all the way to the Gulf. Manuel's mother sighed. What a nice trip, she said. She looked fondly at her husband and then at Manuel.

Manuelito, she asked, do you remember those little villages in Big Bend? Manuel shrugged. No me acuerdo, ma. Manuel's father held out his hand to interject. Well, he said, I remember it like it was yesterday. People would cross back and forth all day long, like the border wasn't even there. He looked at me and raised his eyebrows. Men would even ride their horses across the river, como en las películas del viejo oeste. Manuel's mother smiled. Es cierto, she said, it was just like the movies. She shook her head and looked down at her granddaughters eating their pizza. There weren't so many problems back then, she said. We even used to take our kids to Juárez. We would go for long weekends with the whole family down to the lakes and mountains south of the city. The children loved it there—they fished and played in the water for days. She looked at Manuel. Do you remember, mijo? Manuel handed another slice of pizza down to his daughter. Yes ma, claro. His mother sighed. We don't go there anymore, she said.

ON THE WAY BACK FROM MANUEL'S HOUSE, BETO AND I talked for the first time about our lives before the patrol. He told me how he'd always wanted to be a cop, how he'd gone to school for criminal justice, always knew he wanted to carry a badge and a gun. Growing up outside El Paso, he said, it seemed like the only ones doing well were either getting paid by the cartels or getting paid to take them down. I asked him about school, if he ever thought he'd go back. He shook his head. For me, he said, this is my life now. I've been doing it for almost ten years. I asked him if he'd ever considered leaving the patrol. He stared out over the steering wheel. He had a mortgage, he said, he was still making payments on his car. He couldn't walk away from the money he made unless it was for something just as good. I chuckled. It's hard for me to relate, I said. What do you mean? I live in your fucking backyard, I said. I could walk away from that whenever I want.

Beto explained to me that to move forward, he would need to become a supervisor or transfer to another agency. Where would you go? I asked. He thought for a moment. Did you know the State Department has its own security force? he asked me. The Diplomatic Security Service. They get to fly all over the world. Beto smiled. Now that would be nice. I looked out the window at the concrete city south of the interstate. I've thought about the State Department too, I told him, but not law enforcement. He laughed. You want to be an ambassador, güey? I shrugged. I used to think about the foreign service, I confessed, but that was before the patrol. They've got these scholarship programs though. You can apply to do research in any country you want. Beto stared ahead at the advancing freeway. Qué chingón, he finally said.

We sat for a few minutes. Then Beto looked over at me. So you're looking for a way out? he asked. I shrugged. I'm not even four years in yet. So what? That doesn't mean you don't want to do something else, pendejo. True enough, I said. I looked out the window again. I always imagined I'd go back to school, I told him. I used to think that I'd go for law, political science, something like that. But now

I don't know. When I was in school, I spent all this time studying international relations, immigration, border security. I was always reading about policy and economics, looking at complex academic ways of addressing this big unsolvable problem. When I made the decision to apply for this job, I had the idea that I'd see things in the patrol that would somehow unlock the border for me, you know? I thought I'd come up with all sorts of answers. And then working here, you see so much, you have all these experiences. But I don't know how to put it into context, I don't know where I fit in it all. I have more questions now than ever before. Beto sat glancing at me with short turns of his head. Damn, he finally said, that shit runs deep.

After we exited the freeway Beto began to talk to me about his family. He had grown up on both sides of the river and still had cousins in Juárez. We used to have these big family reunions on the south side, he told me, but now I only see my cousins when they come to El Paso to party. As we neared the house, I asked Beto if he ever went south of the line to see his family. Never, he said. Not since I've been in the patrol. He stopped for a traffic light at the base of a hill and looked down an empty side street. Even before things got really bad, he told me, I still wouldn't go. I knew it would probably be fine, but there's something about being an agent. It just never felt smart. I nodded. I haven't gone either, I told him.

The signal turned green and Beto accelerated up the hill as I wondered to myself what it was, the thing that kept us from crossing to the other side.

IN *ANTÍGONA GONZÁLEZ*, SARA URIBE WRITES:

Count them all.
Name them so as to say: this body could be mine.
The body of one of my own.
So as not to forget that all the bodies without names are our
   lost bodies.

I DREAM THAT I AM IN CIUDAD JUÁREZ WITH MANUEL AND Beto. We are driving at night through a street filled with people, and we park our car along the side of the road to join the crowds. We walk through the city with the people of Juárez, celebrating with them in the open air. I dance with girls in the street, kissing and spinning them in the light. I can sense that there is an unease among the crowd, and every so often Beto leans toward me to point out certain people connected to the cartel, certain vehicles to keep an eye on, certain places to avoid. In the early dawn the crowds thin out and we begin making our way back to our parked vehicle. As we walk along the sidewalk, Manuel gestures behind us. In the distance men can be seen making their way down the road, killing and kidnapping everyone who remains on the streets. They're coming this way, Manuel tells us. We hurry toward the car and I think to myself that we should have known better than to come here. We've all seen the bloody images, I think, why did we come? We reach the car. As we speed through the city, the streets begin to fill once more with people. The city's residents are starting their morning, carrying flowers with them as they walk in all directions. How do they live with the fear, I wonder to myself, how do they survive?

HISTORIAN TIMOTHY SNYDER HAS SPENT MUCH OF HIS career examining the terror waged against the people of Eastern Europe between 1930 and 1945 in the borderlands between World War II–era Germany and the Soviet Union. His book *Bloodlands* chronicles the twin genocides perpetrated by Hitler and Stalin in modern-day Poland, Ukraine, Lithuania, Belarus, and western Russia—campaigns of ethnically and politically motivated mass killing and starvation writ large.

Snyder implores his readers to view the staggering number of deaths—fourteen million—as fourteen million *times one*. "Each record of death," he writes, "suggests, but cannot supply, a unique life. We must be able not only to reckon the number of deaths but to reckon with each victim as an individual." Snyder explains that "to join in a large number after death is to be dissolved into a stream of anonymity. To be enlisted posthumously into competing national memories, bolstered by the numbers of which your life has become a part, is to sacrifice individuality. It is to be abandoned by history."

Snyder ends his book with a plea to academics and fellow historians, to all those who grapple with death on a grand scale. "It is for us as scholars," he urges, "to seek these numbers and to put them into perspective. It is for us as humanists to turn the numbers back into people."

HAYWARD CAME TO MY OFFICE IN THE LATE MORNING WHILE I was reading through the day's news on my computer. Are you busy? he asked. No, I said, looking up from the computer screen. He stared at my face. Jesus, he said, you look like shit. Thanks, I replied. I haven't been sleeping, that's all. Well, he said, let's go grab some lunch.

After ordering Hayward took his hat off and placed it on the table. There was a shooting at your old station, he told me, did you hear? No, I said. What happened? An agent shot and killed a Guatemalan down near the line. Damn, I said. They say it was a good shot, Hayward continued, self-defense, cut-and-dried. What was the agent's name? I asked. Lopez, he said. Do you know him? I thought back to my days at the station. I don't remember a Lopez. Well shit, Hayward replied, I was going to see if you knew how he was doing. He sat back in his seat and gazed out the window. I know how hard it can be on a man after he kills someone, he said after some time. Have the other guys told you about me? I blinked at him in confusion. What do you mean? I asked. I shot a kid once, Hayward said. Back when I was a cop in Virginia. I thought maybe you'd heard. People talk, you know. He held his hat between his hands, bending and shaping the brim.

When the call came out on the radio, Hayward told me, he was on his way back to the station after working a double shift. There was a plainclothes detective just a few blocks away, engaged in a pursuit with a stolen vehicle. Hayward responded with lights and sirens and blocked the vehicle's escape route down a side street. When the car stopped to make a U-turn, the plainclothes detective jumped out of his vehicle and attempted to remove the driver from the stolen car. As he pulled the door open, the driver took his arm and held on to him as he made the turn. Hayward saw that the detective was hanging from the car and being dragged across the pavement as the car accelerated, so he aimed and fired two shots, hitting the driver right in the head. I didn't know where the bullet hit, he said, but I saw the driver go limp and watched the car come to a stop. He was just a kid, seventeen years old. There was a passenger too, a nineteen-year-old, unharmed.

Hayward stared at his hat, an old and quiet pain spreading across his face the likes of which I hoped I would never be made to carry. Hell, Hayward finally said, I was barely in my twenties.

IN THEIR ONGOING ATTEMPTS TO UNDERSTAND THE ROOTS of human violence, scientists have identified a genetic deficiency that predisposes certain men to acts of hostility. In 1978, in the southeastern Dutch city of Nijmegen, a woman approached medical experts at the Radboud University Medical Center, concerned about a history of violence in her family, which included her brothers, her son, and generations of her male forebears. These men raped and abused their sisters, they chased down their employers in rage, they committed arson, they got in fights, they leveled threats against family members, friends, coworkers, and strangers. In 1962 the woman's peaceable grand-uncle, a teacher at an institution for the learning disabled, traced the violence in his family as far back as 1870, identifying nine male family members and ancestors with a history of such behavior. For over a decade, geneticists at the University of Nijmegen conducted research on the woman and her family.

In 1993, after fifteen years of investigation, researchers identified a deficiency in a gene that encodes an enzyme called monoamine oxidase A, or MAOA, a key regulator of impulse control. Individuals with low levels of MAOA, it seemed, were predisposed to violence, and researchers came to refer to them as carriers of a "warrior gene." Since the occurrence of this deficiency is tied to a defect in the X chromosome, men—possessing only one X chromosome, while women possess two—are more prone to the defect, although women may carry it and pass it on to their sons. Subsequent studies revealed that about one-third of the world's male population carry the warrior gene, the expression of which can be triggered by childhood exposure to trauma.

Dr. James Fallon, a neuroscientist at the University of California, Irvine, upon discovering that several of his ancestors had a grisly history of murder, submitted himself to brain scans and genetic analysis. His genetic results and brain activity patterns matched those thought by scientists to be associated with aggression and violence. Fallon attributed his failure to succumb to a "charmed" upbringing. "If you have the high-risk form of the gene and you were abused early on in life," he explained in an interview, "your chances of a life of crime are much higher. If you have the high-risk gene but you weren't abused, then there really wasn't much risk. So just a gene by itself, the variant doesn't really dramatically affect behavior, but under certain environmental conditions there is a big difference."

Dr. Fallon does not specify the environmental conditions that might lead to the activation of the warrior gene, nor does he suggest whether large-scale trauma, enacted over decades across an entire society, might trigger the ceaseless perpetuation of violence. He does not indicate how long our subconscious can absorb terror and fear—how long we can live in proximity to aggression and cruelty—before slipping into madness.

I AGREED TO TAKE CARE OF BETO'S DOG WHILE HE WAS deployed for several days on an intelligence mission out of town. Before he left I told him that I planned to hike in the Franklin Mountains over the weekend. Can your dog handle a steep climb and a few hours of walking? I asked. Probably not, Beto said.

In the morning, before leaving for the hike, I fed Beto's dog and left him in the gated backyard. As I drove through El Paso to the Mc-Kelligon Canyon trailhead on the east side of the mountains, I noticed a heavy spring wind blowing across the city. The wind tore at my shirt as I climbed up the canyon, the dust obscuring the views to the east.

An hour later, at the top of a peak, I looked out to see the entire region covered by a massive cloud of gray-brown dust. On a clear day I would have been able to see the West Texas plains and the deserts of New Mexico, I would have been able to look south across the city of Juárez and the surrounding countryside of Chihuahua, but with the blowing dust I couldn't even see to the base of the mountains. I made my way back down the canyon spitting dirt and shielding my eyes.

I returned home to find the gate to the backyard slung open and Beto's dog missing. In the fading dust-filtered light of the evening, I drove frantically through the surrounding neighborhood searching for the dog, unable to see more than a hundred yards in front of me. Through the brown haze I saw a woman walking down the street with a hooded sweatshirt pulled tight around her face. I rolled down the window and shouted to her over the wind. The dog catcher came through here maybe fifteen minutes ago, she told me. I drove back to Beto's house to find an impoundment notice from El Paso Animal Services on the door. I raced across town to the shelter, cursing myself aloud.

At the shelter I found Beto's dog covered in blood and bite marks, cowering in the corner of the kennel. I felt, briefly, as if I were in a nightmare. He was in a fight, the officer explained. He'll be fine, but he messed the other dog up pretty good. The officer gave me the address of a house a few blocks down the street and I drove straight there, leaving Beto's dog curled in the passenger seat of my truck. Standing in front of the house, I wondered why I shouldn't just turn around and leave, why I should hold myself responsible for a fight that wasn't mine. At the door I was met by a disheveled woman. I was supposed to be watching the dog, I told her, losing my words. I placed a hand over my chest and clenched my jaw. The woman stood with her hand still gripping the doorknob. Is your dog all right? I finally asked. My husband took her to the animal clinic, she said, barely concealing her anger. Your fucking dog tore her throat open, right through the goddamned jugular. I lowered my gaze. She's getting stitches, the woman said, we don't know if she'll make it. She stared at me with eyes wide and unblinking. I'm sorry, I told her. We stood with coldness between us until, finally, I turned to leave. I'll come back for the vet bills, I told her, I promise.

That night, as dust blew across the desert, I kneeled in the backyard of Beto's home, trembling as I washed blood from the face of an animal.

IN HIS BOOK *WHAT HAVE WE DONE*, VETERAN WAR REPORTER David Wood examines the pervasiveness of "moral injury" among soldiers who have returned from the battlefronts in Iraq and Afghanistan. Long confused with PTSD, moral injury is a more subtle wound, characterized not by flashbacks or a startle complex but by "sorrow, remorse, grief, shame, bitterness, and moral confusion" that manifest not in physical reactions but in emotional responses as subtle as dreams and doubts. "In its most simple and profound sense," writes Wood, "moral injury is a jagged disconnect from our understanding of who we are and what we and others ought to do and ought not to do." As a soldier tells him, "Moral injury is a learned behavior, learning to accept the things you know are wrong."

Wood describes how "most of us . . . have a firm and deeply personal understanding of life's moral rules, of justice and injustice, right and wrong. That sense, our inner compass, is built on beliefs we begin to acquire as infants . . . But war, by its very nature, tends to suddenly and violently upend these remaining moral beliefs. Things don't go well in war, whose very purpose demands death and destruction." This upending is often a gradual process, one that is difficult to perceive. Likewise, moral injury is a wound that sets in slowly, something that occurs, as one Iraq veteran wrote, "when a person has time to reflect on a traumatic experience."

When Wood writes of moral injury, he refers most often to traumas suffered in combat, by soldiers deployed in foreign war zones on the other side of the earth. But he also notes that one does not have to be in combat to suffer from moral injury. He reminds us that war is something that reaches far beyond the battlefield, something that leaches out into proximate geographies and relationships, seeping deep into the individual and societal unconscious. "To be in war," Wood states, even in this broader sense, "is to be exposed to moral injury."

OUR TEAM WAS DEPLOYED TO WORK A MISSION IN THE DESerts of my old station. Before we left El Paso, Hayward came to me to say he needed me at my best. You know the lay of the land. I want you out there helping Manuel to triangulate scout locations, matching up the intercepted communications with what you know from the ground, what you see on the maps. I want to know where they're staging their loads and what they can see from their lookout points. There's a shit ton of dope moving through here—let's figure out where it's headed.

I rode through long days with Manuel and Beto, gazing out the window at the blossoming landscape, bright with green creosote and yellow plumes of palo verde, with red-tipped ocotillos and endless orange wildflowers. As we listened to crackling voices on the scanners, I imagined that I might know where they were and I tried to hold in my mind their high-up views across the ephemeral lushness of the desert.

In the late afternoons we returned to the forward operating base where we had set up a trailer to serve as our mobile command center. One evening, a few hours before sundown, Hayward suggested that some of us take ATVs down the back roads to survey the approach to a nearby scout hill. You guys go, I told him, I'll stay back and work on the shift report. Half an hour after leaving with Manuel and Beto, Hayward called me on my cell phone. We ran across a quitter, he said, can you transport her back to the base for us? Sure, I said. I asked if she was all right, if she had water. She's fine, he assured me.

When I arrived I saw Hayward, Manuel, and Beto standing over a small woman sitting in the middle of the dirt road. Hayward walked over to me as Beto and Manuel continued speaking with the

THE LINE BECOMES A RIVER

woman in Spanish. We checked her pockets, he said, this is all she had. He handed me a cell phone. Her group left her behind. Looks like she's got a pretty bad limp—probably has some nasty blisters. Manuel and Beto walked the woman to the back of my patrol vehicle and helped her into the backseat. Vete con cuidado, señora, Manuel told her before shutting the door. I looked up at the sky and then at Hayward. You should get going, I told him, there's not much daylight left. Whatever you say, boss, he said. Just don't forget that report.

As I drove down the dirt road back toward the base, I looked at the woman in the rearview mirror through the mesh of the metal cage that separated us. I tried to think of something to say but found myself unable to speak. Is it all right if I roll down the windows? I finally asked. Lo que usted quiere, oficial. I rolled the windows down and turned to look at the woman. Me puedes tutear, I told her.

Cool air blew in from outside and I gazed beyond the road at the dust devils creeping across the warmly lit valley, a myriad of clay-colored cones whirling in the distance. For a short time, driving down the open road, I felt a strange and familiar sense of freedom, an old closeness with the desert. Perhaps there was something comforting, I thought, about being able look out across the landscape and see for myself the horrors laid upon it. I looked again through the mesh to the woman seated behind me. She stared out the open window, her hair whipping at her sun-wrinkled face. I wondered what she might have seen, what she might feel looking out at the desert, and I was certain it was no sense of freedom.

At the forward operating base I parked and helped the woman out of the vehicle. I offered her my arm as she limped up the walkway to a small holding area. Inside, she sat on a cold steel bench as I asked her a series of questions to fill out her voluntary return papers, the only semblance of conversation I was able to have with her. I'm forty-six years old, she told me. I was trying to get to Phoenix to see my husband. My group crossed four days ago. They left me after the second day. I come from Guerrero.

After filling out the paperwork I asked the woman if I could see her feet. I'm an EMT, I told her, I can tell you how bad they are. She took her shoes off slowly, embarrassed at the smell. It's all right, I said, I've smelled it before. As she removed her socks, the fabric, stiff with days of dried sweat, pulled at the skin of her soles. The balls and heels of her feet were covered with silver-dollar-sized blisters. I opened a medical kit and put on a pair of gloves. I touched her feet, turning them slowly in my hands. They're okay, I assured her, I've seen worse. Most of your blisters are unbroken.

I cleaned her feet one at a time with a disinfectant wipe, swabbing the fluid from the edges of her broken blisters and smearing them with ointment. Slowly, I unraveled a roll of white gauze around each pallid foot, then covered them gently with an elastic wrap. As I looked up, I saw that the woman had been watching me with her head resting on her shoulder. Eres muy humanitario, oficial, she told me. I looked down at her feet and shook my head. No, I said, I'm not.

154

"THE HORRIBLE THING IS WHEN YOU ARE DREAMING," THE sicario tells his interviewers. "You have very realistic dreams. I would dream that I was running through the streets, jumping over cars. Oh, I would dream that I was out there and did not have my weapon and they were chasing me. And the dreams were so real that I would wake up and the gun was on the pillow and I would have my weapon in my hand and I would be aiming it.

"I was very violent," the sicario explains. "The dreams are not things that could never happen, they are not fantastic dreams, but very realistic. The fear that I had that kept me from sleeping in my house with my family, the reason I would go someplace to sleep by myself . . . it was because the least little noise would cause you to react violently . . . One time my wife tried to help me when I was dreaming . . . She saw I was having a nightmare and tried to wake me up, but when she touched me—*ARRRGGH*—my reaction was to grab her by the throat . . . I was strangling her, I was strangling my own wife." The sicario's huge hands tremble as he makes a gesture of strangulation, his fingers stretched out and quivering.

"From that moment," he says, "that very moment, I realized that something very bad was happening to me. I was no longer any good. There was a line that I had respected between the work I did—as a guard, as an instructor, as an executioner—but this work no longer stayed on one side of the line."

Events like this finally led him to leave the business of killing. "During your trajectory through life," he explains, "there comes a moment when you hit a roadblock, you reach your limit." To sever ties with the cartel, the sicario fled with his family and began a life in hiding, a life that would be plagued with a new and unwavering fear. He accepted a friend's invitation to accompany him to a prayer service at a Christian church. "My surprise was, as soon as I got there . . . I don't know what I felt. I really can't explain this feeling. I just started to cry." In the film, the sicario begins to weep as he tells the story. His head, enveloped by the black hood, rocks gently, his voice quavers. "I did not hear the preaching," he says, "I did not hear anything . . . I fell to crying, I cried as I had never cried, more than I ever remember crying in my childhood . . . I cried for five or six hours without stopping. Kneeling down, falling down on the floor . . . And I heard the people crying for me. And I felt their hands touching me . . . I could feel the warmth of them touching me."

BETWEEN DEPLOYMENTS HAYWARD SCHEDULED OUR TEAM to spend a morning at the firing range to satisfy our quarterly firearms qualification. After completing the course of fire alongside Manuel and Beto, I asked Hayward if I could speak to him alone. We walked out to the parking lot and stood beside his patrol vehicle. I looked at the ground and he crossed his arms. What's up? he asked. I was accepted for a research scholarship to study abroad, I finally told him. I'm going to take it. It's a good opportunity for me. Damn, Hayward said. Congratulations. That's great for you. I kicked at the gravel beneath my feet. I need out for a while, I confessed. I looked up and held my hand out to block the sun from my eyes. I've been wanting to study again, I told him, I'm thinking about a master's degree. Hayward stared off into the distance, squinting at the mountains. I hate to lose you, he said.

As we walked back toward the firing range I told him how much I liked working for him, how much I liked being on the team, how much I'd learned from everyone. We stopped at the edge of the parking lot and Hayward stood in thought. You know, he said, we could offer you a leave of absence. You could do your time abroad and come back and take classes on the side. There's even a program to support agents getting their degree—we can find a way for you to stay on if you want. I remained silent for a moment, clenching my teeth. I can't, I wanted to tell him, it's not the work for me.

"WHAT MEXICANS IN THE EARLY TWENTY-FIRST CENTURY have been forced to see," writes poet and essayist Cristina Rivera Garza, "is without a doubt one of the most chilling spectacles of contemporary horrorism." In her book *Dolerse*—the title is the Spanish verb meaning "to be in pain"—she attempts to construct and deconstruct the pervasiveness of pain in modern Mexican society. "Pain is a complex phenomenon which, in the first place, calls into question our most basic notions of what constitutes reality," she writes. "Pain not only destroys, but produces reality." The "social languages" of pain are, in fact, "political languages" as well, "languages in which bodies decipher their power relationships with other bodies." Thus, at a political and social level, she argues, "the language of pain becomes a producer of meanings and legitimacy."

Pain, of course, is intimately linked with fear. "Fear isolates," writes Rivera Garza. "Fear teaches us to distrust. Fear makes us crazy." If we follow the arc of her argument, we see that pain has the power to destroy and to produce its own reality, a reality in turn legitimized and given further meaning through the politics and policies that shape our society. This reality is quite often a reality of fear, a reality that makes us—individually and as a society—crazy, isolated, filled with distrust for our fellow human beings, the people who share our neighborhoods, our cities, our country, our borders, our intractably and intimately interwoven global community— the people with whom we share our very lives.

In her essay "War and Imagination," Rivera Garza considers the work of Italian writer and cultural critic Alessandro Baricco. "He claimed that war has always existed," she writes, "in the very bones of a vast range of different civilizations: the adrenaline of war, the excitation of war, the hypnotic song of war. It is only when we, as societies, are able to invent something more exciting, more risky, more adventurous, more revolutionary, that we can say we are truly against war." She calls this "a form of radical pacifism."

Taking her cue from Baricco, Rivera Garza declares: "If we want to move beyond war based in fear, the purpose of which is to produce more fear, we'd do better to imagine something more exciting, more extreme; something even more wholly filled with adrenaline." After all, "the person who imagines always might imagine that this, whatever this might be, can be different . . . The person who imagines knows, and knows from within, that nothing is natural. Nothing inevitable."

I DREAM THAT I AM OUT WORKING IN THE DESERT, THAT I have stopped a vehicle on the shoulder of an empty highway. As I walk toward the vehicle, a long-haired man and a boy step out of the car and walk toward me. I see that the man has a gun and I shout at him to drop it. The man continues walking toward me and I reach for my sidearm, desperate for some element of control. I aim my weapon at the center of his body and yell for him to let go of his gun. He holds the weapon in his hand and looks at the boy. Then, before he turns again to look at me, I shoot him in the chest. His gun falls and slides across the ground and I shoot him again, over and over, firing five shots from my weapon. When I look up from the dead man's body I see that the boy has taken the gun and is crouched and aiming at me from behind the car. He shoots at me and misses. I turn and aim at him, gripping the gun with both hands. I fire at the boy twice, hitting him once in the head and once in the shoulder. I look at the scene before me and am gripped with profound panic. A crushing darkness washes over everything and I throw my gun to the ground, terrified that I have become forever looped in a crippling exchange of violence. I think that I should call Hayward, that

I should call my mother, and then I turn to look for the body of the dead man. I go over to make sure the body is still there, to see for certain that the man is dead. As I stand over him, moving his arm with the toe of my boot, I hear the boy struggling for air next to the car. I walk over and stand above his body, trying to understand how he could still be breathing. I'm alive, the boy gasps, looking at my face. Please kill me, he says, please finish it. I stand and look down at the boy in silence before finally turning to walk away.

Upon waking, I sit up in my bed and weep. I wish to make the sign of the cross, to offer out my hand. "Brother wolf," I wish to say, "I will make peace between us, O brother wolf."

III

oday," Carl Jung wrote near the end of his life, "we are again living in an age filled with apocalyptic images of universal destruction." Jung was addressing what had become, after the conclusion of World War II, the defining conflict of the times. As he saw it, the cold war reflected the state of modern humanity's psyche, with the Iron Curtain as its prevailing symbol. "This boundary line bristling with barbed wire," he wrote, "runs through the psyche of modern man, no matter on which side he lives." Even "the normal individual . . . sees his shadow in his neighbor or in the man beyond the great divide." Jung went so far as to assert that it had become "a political and social duty" to perceive "the other as the very devil, so as to fascinate the outward eye and prevent it from looking at the individual life within."

In Jung's view, "the mass State"—his term for government and its structures—has "no intention of promoting mutual understanding and the relationship of man to man; it strives, rather, for atomization, for the psychic isolation of the individual." Jung asserts that when we come to perceive "the other" as someone to be feared and shunned, we risk the inner cohesion of our society, allowing our personal relationships to become undermined by a creeping mistrust. By walling ourselves off from a perceived other, we "flatter the primitive tendency in us to shut our eyes to evil and drive it over some frontier or other, like the Old Testament scapegoat, which was supposed to carry the evil into the wilderness."

The effort to push away our individual and societal shadows is undertaken in the hope that we might "quickly and conveniently sink into the sea of forgetfulness" and reclaim a sense of normalcy, however vague and distorted. But in reality, Jung warns, "nothing has finally disappeared and nothing has been made good. The evil, the guilt, the profound unease of conscience, the obscure misgivings are there before our eyes, if only we would see." Jung urges us, instead, to recognize the selfsame nature of the other, to declare, "I am guilty with the rest," to understand that "none of us stands outside humanity's black collective shadow," and ultimately to accept evil as something "lodged in human nature itself . . . as the equal and opposite partner of good."

In his work as a psychologist, Jung argued against the division of the psyche, the dissociation between good and evil, the bifurcation between the conscious and unconscious selves. The goal of psychoanalytic therapy, as he saw it, was not to bring life into some sort of harmony, but to engage in a process he called "individuation," the opening up of a dialogue between our waking consciousness and the often repressed preoccupations of our unconscious mind. He saw individuation as a path toward discerning wholeness in seemingly irreconcilable opposites, a way of holding darkness within the psyche, a way of learning to live with the chaos and disorder of our lives.

For Jung, understanding dreams was an essential part of this process. "Dreams are the guiding words of the soul," he wrote. "Dreams pave the way for life, and they determine you without you understanding their language." If the events of our waking lives were filtered and given an extra layer of meaning through dreams, then the unconscious held essential clues for coming to terms with hidden anxieties and preoccupations. "The dream describes the inner situation of the dreamer," he wrote, "but the conscious mind denies its truth and reality, or admits it only grudgingly." In order to begin a true reckoning with our inner situation, "we have to expose ourselves to the animal impulses of the unconscious without identifying with them and without 'running away.'"

To illustrate his point, Jung offered the following example: "When you dream of a savage bull, or a lion, or a wolf . . . this means: it wants to come to you. You would like to split it off, you experience it as something alien—but it just becomes all the more dangerous. The urge of what had been split off to unite with you becomes all the stronger. The best stance would be: 'Please, come and devour me.'"

I arrived at the coffee shop each morning at six-thirty, half an hour before the first customers. I ground pre-weighed beans and started the drip machine, filling three insulated airpots with coffee. I dialed in the espresso grind, weighing and timing each shot until I got the right yield, the right ratio of grounds in to liquid out. I turned on the water tower. I displayed bags of whole-bean craft-roasted coffee in neatly arranged rows. I set up a pour-over station, with scales and glass carafes and ceramic V60 drippers made in Japan. I unlocked the retail refrigerator, full of Italian sodas and green glass bottles of sparkling water. I set out the chocolate and vanilla and caramel syrups, I filled an insulated pitcher with organic half-and-half and restocked the to-go station with hot sleeves, stir sticks, straws, lids, napkins, and raw sugar packets. I walked across the courtyard to fetch ice from the commercial kitchen. Then I unfolded the wooden shop sign in the courtyard, removed the "closed" placard from the countertop, opened the register, and set out my tip jar.

The coffee shop was one of many retail outlets in a shared marketplace, a small business complex situated around an open-air courtyard in the style of an old Spanish mercado. At six-thirty in the morning I encountered few other workers as I puttered about: the pastry chefs at the Mexican bakery, the prep cooks at the taco shop, and the maintenance man who maintained the mercado grounds—a strong and clean-shaven man from Oaxaca named José, dressed always in a black baseball hat and a gray T-shirt stretched taut across his broad shoulders and tucked neatly into a pair of black jeans. José would clean the surface of the courtyard with a garden hose or a long-handled push broom. He regularly cleared the adjacent sidewalks with a leaf blower, rippling small waves of debris toward the street gutters to be swept away by monsoon rains and hot summer winds. He arranged the courtyard furniture, unlocked doors with the keys dangling from his waist, punched in codes to disarm the security system, and opened the gates of the mercado to let in the day's first customers.

José and I often talked to each other across the counter of the coffee bar in the early hours before the morning rush. We spoke in Spanish, exchanging cordialities. He asked about my graduate studies, about my travel plans, about my luck with women. He asked about my family, and I asked about his. He asked about my mother, about the health of her heart, and he would ask that I greet her on his behalf when I left the city to visit her. I asked him, in turn, about his wife and three boys. He stood proudly with his arm resting on the countertop the day his oldest son started high school, smiled broadly the day his youngest boy won his first soccer tournament, and leaned infirmly on a broom handle the day his middle son was hit by a car. He's getting better, he would say for months after the accident, gracias a Dios.

JOSÉ KNEW I HAD SPENT SEVERAL YEARS IN THE BORDER
Patrol, but he rarely questioned me about the work, almost as if there
were not much to ask. Likewise, I relinquished certain questions
about his arrival and status. In my day-to-day interactions with
migrants—the customers at the coffee shop, the workers I encountered throughout the city, the day laborers who came to the park to
play pick-up soccer with my friends and me in the evenings—I often
recognized subtle marks left by the crossing of the border, an understanding of its physical and abstract dimensions, a lingering impression of its weight. I sensed this knowledge in José as well, but there
was little way to speak of something so imprecise, and so we regarded
each other with nods and silences, with glances and gestures, with
something that soon became friendship.

One day, as I stood counting tips at the end of my shift, José
pulled up a chair at the bar and sat to drink from a bottle of sparkling water. As I changed out a pile of singles for a twenty-dollar
bill, I could feel his eyes resting on me. I looked up at him and he
motioned for me to come near. Oye, he said in a hushed tone, when
you were in la migra you must have made good money, qué no?
Sure, I said. He looked around to make sure no one was within ear-
shot and then leaned closer. More money than you make here, qué
no? I laughed. Claro que sí. He leaned back in his chair, confused.
Entonces por qué lo dejaste? I shrugged, somehow surprised that he

had finally asked. In the end, I said, it wasn't the work for me. I avoided his eyes, thinking of what more to add. Finally I looked up at him. I wanted to go back to school, I said, study writing, earn a master's degree. José gave me a mischievous grin. A student doesn't make much money, he said. I chuckled and gestured at the small pile of tips on the counter. He looked at me unbelievingly. You could make more somewhere else. But I like the pace, I said, and the people are nice. I pointed at the espresso machine. The coffee's good too. José laughed. Claro, he said. Todo el mundo necesita café.

José continued to look at me curiously. Why study writing? he asked. Why not business, medicine, politics? Así podrías ganar más dinero. I shrugged again. Writing seemed like a good way to make sense of what I'd seen. José sat back in his chair. Ah. Ahora te entiendo, he said. I could write many books, he added after a while. He visto muchas cosas.

JOSÉ AND I OFTEN SPOKE OF THE DRUG WARS AND THE disorder swirling in Mexico—the forty-three students who disappeared in Ayotzinapa, the endless cartel shootouts along the border, the persistent corruption of police and government officials. One day he told a joke. There was this big deer-hunting contest, he began, with hunters from the U.S., Russia, and Mexico. On the first day, the Americans came triumphantly before the judges, but the carcass they presented was so destroyed by their high-powered weaponry that it was unrecognizable as a deer, so they were disqualified. On the second day, the Russians brought in the body of a large buck, but when the judges discovered the animal had been poisoned instead of properly hunted, they too were disqualified. A third and a fourth day passed and still there was no sign of the Mexicans. On the fifth day, the judges finally decided to go looking for them. After several hours of searching, they found them in a clearing in the woods, huddled around a rabbit. One of them was torturing the animal without mercy, while another stood over it, shouting: Confess you're a deer, motherfucker!

On the day the Mexican military captured El Chapo Guzmán in 2014, José asked me, Do you think it's really him? I don't know, I replied, do you? I'm not sure. He has body doubles, you know? José paused. Or maybe the government made arrangements to arrest someone who looks just like him. Several days later, José showed me pictures that had turned up on the Internet—zoomed-in images of the drug lord's face side-by-side with pictures from his prior arrest in 1993. Se ve diferente, he said, qué no? I studied them. Puede ser, I offered. He set his phone on the counter and stared at one of the photos. He doesn't really look like a drug lord, he said. No se ve tan malo. I poured him a cup of coffee and leaned against my end of the counter. You never know, I told him. Violent people look like everyone else.

José looked up at me. When you were on the border, he asked, did you ever find drugs? Sure, I told him. More than you can imagine. He nodded slowly, his eyes unblinking. Did you ever arrest a narco? Sure, I said. But not like El Chapo. José listened intently. We mostly arrested the little people—smugglers, scouts, mules, coyotes. I watched as a knowing look spread across his face. His eyes met mine and held them until I turned to look away. But mostly I arrested migrants, I confessed. People looking for a better life.

AROUND NINE OR TEN IN THE MORNING, EVERY DAY WITH-out fail, José brought his breakfast to the coffee bar and sat at the counter to eat. He ate the same thing each morning, a vegetarian breakfast burrito from the taco shop next door, and every morning he offered to share it with me. Vas a querer burro? he would ask, and most mornings I would accept. Grab a knife, he'd say, cut it in half, take however much you want. I made him coffee in exchange, al-ways in a paper cup, flavored with a shot of vanilla and a splash of half-and-half. He often commented on the quality of the burrito: it's good today, the beans are cold, there's too much salt, there must be a new cook. He would comment on the salsa: it's watery today, it's not spicy enough. Sometimes he would even come to me before ordering: I could order black beans instead of pintos, I could add avocado, qué te parece?

Some days José would offer to split a dessert with me, donuts or yellow cake from the bakery next door. One morning, he brought in breakfast made by his wife, comida típica de Oaxaca, he told me. He offered me as much as I wanted—I eat like this all the time, he said, smiling. As I ate from his Tupperware, I told him I had once arrested two men from Oaxaca. José's eyes grew wide. Oh, sí?

he asked. They were good people, I told him, gente humilde. José smiled. Así somos en Oaxaca. They shared their food with me just like this, I told him. I described the beef jerky, the grasshoppers, the dried fish. José beamed, his eyes hungry and sparkling. Carne seca, he said, chapulines, charales. But the best part, I continued, was the mezcal they gave me, made by their father right there in their village. José sat back and opened his mouth. Ahhhh, he said, el mezcal es muy bueno.

José leaned on the counter and shook his head, looking down at the wood grain. Yo antes tomaba mucho mezcal. My cousin, he makes his own mezcal, he harvests the maguey from around our village. We used to drink it straight from the still. He gazed out the window and across the courtyard. Fui alcohólico, he admitted quietly. He straightened his back. Pero ya no, he told me, I've been sober for fifteen years, ever since my first son was born.

Day after day, month after month, every morning at the coffee shop was the same. José would complete his daily tasks and then come to the counter to talk and share his food. For nearly two years there wasn't a single day he didn't come, not a single day he didn't sit down and offer to break bread with me.

ONE MORNING I ASKED JOSÉ ABOUT HIS HOME IN OAXACA. His village was small, he told me, nestled in the jungled mountains south of the capital. It's peaceful there, he said—so far the violence hasn't come for us. Where I'm from the people are humble and hardworking. There's little money to be had, he said, but in my village the people still haven't turned to drugs and killing.

Later that morning, during a lull in business, he came to the counter with his smartphone. He opened Google Earth and spread his fingers across the screen, bringing close the state of Oaxaca, the green hills surrounding his village. He smiled longingly at the satellite image, pointing to neatly cultivated fields at the settlement's edge. This is where my cousins make their mezcal, he told me with glinting eyes. In Street View he pointed at colored buildings and cracked roads. This is the church, he said, his voice far-off and trailing, this is the municipal plaza. I interrupted our conversation to refill coffee mugs, to take the order of a customer, but each time José remained at the counter, absorbed in his phone. Look, he called to me, it's my mother's house. I walked over and he pressed his finger at the screen. You can tell by the arches. He sat back in his chair, smiling.

THE FIRST TIME MY MOTHER TOOK ME TO MEXICO I WAS just a boy, still unable to grasp and file away memories. She took me by train through the state of Chihuahua to a place called Casas Grandes, site of the ancient Mogollon settlement of Paquimé. I wanted to go to Mexico with my little boy, she would later tell me, because I wanted him to grow up knowing the border, to see it as a place of power, a place of discovery.

My mother had just separated from my father and was seeking to prove to herself that she did not need protection, that she could travel as a single woman in a way that trusted people, in a way that imparted this trust to her son. When we arrived at the town near the ruins, my mother took me to a market next to the station and asked the man working there if he knew of a place where we could stay. My mother remembers how the man smiled at her without menace, how he referred to her—for the first time in her life—as señora instead of señorita. He wrote down the name and address of a woman with a guesthouse nearby. She doesn't like to take in many people, he said, but she'll take in a mother and her child.

Later that afternoon, after leaving our belongings at the guest-house, my mother remembers going with me to a small plaza. She remembers that there were women and children there, that the women greeted her warmly, that one woman even gave her a hug before bending down to speak to me in Spanish. The woman introduced me to her little boy and we ran off together to play on the steps of the gazebo as my mother joined the other women. My mother tells me that never before had she felt so accepted by a group of women. She describes the moment as transcendent. It didn't matter that her Spanish was poor, that she came as a tourist from another country. It didn't matter, she says, because we were mothers.

The next day, the man from the market drove us to the ruins of Paquimé. When we arrived my mother found that the park was closed for archaeological work. But the men who worked there, see-ing that she was a mother, seeing that she had come from so far away with a small child, welcomed us to walk through the ruins. As we walked I became fascinated by the men at work. Before long, I was improvising a game of cowboys and Indians. I would hide behind a rock near the workmen and then pop up with my arms outstretched and my fingers pointed at them. I would make the noise *boom*. My mother remembers how one man stopped what he was doing to clutch his chest and fall backward, feigning death. She remembers how I laughed with delight. She remembers how another man threw down his tools to jump behind an ancient mud wall. He popped up with his fingers aimed at me. *Boom*, he said, and I jumped back in surprise.

My mother still remembers how I ran laughing through the labyrinthine ruins that afternoon, chasing and hiding from the workers. She remembers losing sight of me but remaining calm. She remembers trusting me, trusting the place, trusting the people around us.

ON A BLAZING SUMMER DAY I NOTICED THAT JOSÉ HAD NOT come to work. Late in the morning the owner of the mercado, a woman named Diane, came in for her daily latte. I asked her if she had heard from José. He called me last night, she said. His mother is dying, poor thing. He's taking two weeks off to go to Oaxaca so he can see her before she passes. She took a sip of her latte and looked out the open door to the courtyard. I know what it's like, she said. I was with my mother the night she died. She passed in her sleep, bless her heart. Diane gazed up at the ceiling. You know, she said, it was the saddest thing, but it was so important for me to be there. She looked back across the counter at me and I struggled to find something to say. Diane shook her head. I'm sorry, she said, I just feel so bad for José, he's such a sweet man. She took another sip of her latte. And I'll tell you what, he's the best worker we've ever had. She held up a finger. In three years of working for me, this is the very first day he's ever missed.

A couple of weeks later, as Diane sat at the bar drinking another latte, I asked her if there was news from José. She glanced at the customers seated on either side of her. He's still in Oaxaca, she told me, tending to his mother's estate. Oh, I said. Later in the day, as I was restocking the supply closet, she called to me from the open door, asking me to come outside.

We walked to the dirt parking lot and I stood with Diane under the glaring summer sun. I didn't want to say this in front of your customers, she began, but I think José is having problems getting back into the country. What kind of problems? I said. She looked into the distance. I don't think he has papers, she told me—we never asked. I shook my head and looked down at the dirt. I wish I could have talked to him before he left. There's nothing you could have said, she told me. Trust me, there was no stopping him. I looked back up at Diane. He doesn't know, I said, getting back across isn't what it used to be. I turned and stared out at the parked cars, squinting against the sun.

Is there any way to get ahold of him? I asked. I can give you his family's number, Diane told me. The last I heard he was at the border, trying to get across. Oh no, I said. He can't cross now. Not in the summer. Diane looked at me. I have to talk to him, I said. I closed my eyes and saw images of volcanic stone and swollen bodies, of hospital sheets and blackened skin. No, I whispered, not José.

WHEN I CALLED THE HOUSE, A SMALL BOY ANSWERED. I introduced myself as a friend of José's. Are you his son? I asked. The boy said nothing. I work with your dad, I continued. I heard he's at the border, trying to get across. Is he okay? After a long silence the boy finally spoke. Do you want my mom to call you? he asked. Sure, I said, and then he hung up.

Half an hour later my phone rang. Soy Lupe, the woman on the other line said, esposa de José. I introduced myself again as a friend from work and told her I was wondering about José. Lupe was silent, as if considering what to say next, how much to tell me. I wanted to blurt out that it was too hot, that it wasn't worth risking his life, that he must wait to cross. It's funny you called, she finally said, because I just got off the phone with the Mexican consulate. They called to tell me José was arrested two days ago by Border Patrol. He has a court hearing later today, at two. They didn't tell me where. I paced with the phone in my hand, pressing it hard against my ear. Lupe's voice sounded thin, as if it were all she could do just to repeat what had been said to her. Today at two? I asked. Yes, she confirmed. I continued pacing in my home, old procedures and timelines rising up in my mind. I think I know where he'll be, I told her. Can I call you back?

IT HAD BEEN MONTHS SINCE I HAD SEEN OR TALKED TO Morales, but I called him anyway. Hey, vato, do you still work at the courthouse? I asked. Simon, he said, but not today. Por qué? I think I have a friend who's getting Streamlined, I said. Shit, a few years out of the patrol and suddenly all your friends are mojados? I tried to think of a comeback. I'm just kidding, Morales said before I could reply—I know how it is. Of course you do, I shot back at him, did you think I forgot you're from Douglas? Shit, you could be a mojado yourself and not even know it. You better not forget to wear your uniform when you show up to court, güey, they might deport your ass. Oh damn, Morales laughed, shots fired!

I asked Morales if Streamline proceedings were still open to the public. Yeah, he said, hippies and protesters come all the time. You never had to go to court? No, I said. Well, you know where the courthouse is, downtown? Go to the second floor, the main courtroom—and be there by one-thirty. I looked at my watch. Will I be able to see him? I asked. Sure, Morales said, if you can pick him out. There'll probably be thirty or forty guys today, and everyone will be facing away from you, pendejo. Can his family come? I asked. Sure, he said. I don't know if they're documented, I told him. It shouldn't matter, he assured me, no one will mess with them. Will they be able to talk to him? I asked. No, Morales answered matter-of-factly. But if you sit on the right-hand side of the courtroom, in the front two rows next to the wall, you should be able to catch his eye as the marshals walk him out.

LUPE AND I MET FOR THE FIRST TIME OUTSIDE THE COURT-room. She came with the pastor from her church and her three boys—fifteen, ten, and eight years old, all of them called out from school in hopes of seeing their father in court. I held the door of the courtroom open for the family and gestured toward the benches against the right wall. The front rows, I whispered. The proceedings had begun just as we entered the courtroom, and I immediately noticed the smell—a smell I had not encountered in years, the sharp scent of dozens of unwashed bodies that had for days struggled through the desert, skin sweating and sunbaked. The courtroom was cathedral-like, with towering ceilings of brightly colored beams painted in turquoise and coral. From his bench the judge loomed over the room, a small white face emerging from black robes and seated beneath the massive seal of the United States of America, a giant eagle with its head turned as if to look away.

I sat next to Lupe, who held her youngest son close to her body with her oldest son seated beside him. Behind us the pastor sat with the middle son. The judge addressed the forty-some defendants seated before him, most of them male, all of them wearing black headsets, listening to the words of an interpreter. All of you have been charged with two crimes, the judge began. I understand that each of you intends to plead guilty to the petty offense of illegal entry at a place other than one designated for entry by U.S. Immigration. In exchange for your plea, the government has agreed to dismiss the felony offense of reentry after removal. Some of the men hunched over, holding the headsets close to their ears. It is important that you understand this, the judge continued. If you understand, please indicate so by standing. He paused. All the men stood, some rising up from their chairs with their shoulders back and their heads held high as if in defiance, while others seemed barely able to get up from their seats, their bodies slumped, their faces downcast.

The maximum penalty for this charge is six months in prison and a $5,000 fine, the judge went on, but the government has agreed to waive this fine in exchange for your plea today. I caught the eye of a Border Patrol agent, who glared at me as if I were somehow allied against him. I stared at his green uniform, at the badge on his chest, the gun on his belt, the iron-creased lines running down his sleeves. You must understand, the judge continued, that in the future this charge will always be used against you, that if you are arrested attempting to reenter the country, you could serve years in prison, not days or months.

I leaned over to Lupe. Do you see José? I asked. I don't know, she said, I can't see their faces. Next to her, her youngest son nervously kicked his dangling legs back and forth. She placed her hand gently on his thigh. Tranquilo, she whispered into his hair. On the floor of the courtroom, the defendants began to file out of their chairs five at a time. Their ankles were chained to one another and their wrists were bound at the waist. They stood before the judge, flanked by court-appointed attorneys—dizzied men and women darting from one client to another in pale suits. The judge began with the person standing to his left. Mr. Amaya, he read, as if from a script: Are you a citizen of Mexico? Sí. On or about August 31, 2015, did you enter the United States near Lukeville, Arizona? Sí. Did you come through a designated port of entry? No. How do you plead in the charge of illegal entry? Culpable, señor.

After repeating this set of questions for each defendant, the judge issued his sentence—for most, thirty days of incarceration in the state detention center an hour north of the city, with credit for time served. One woman, after answering the judge's questions, interrupted before he issued her sentence. I'm pregnant, señor, she said. The judge paused. He looked around, as if for guidance. I'll put a note in your file, he said, for someone to see you at the facility.

Watching the defendants shuffle to the front of the room to stand before the bench, I realized that I had never before seen so many men and women in shackles, that I had never laid eyes on a group of people so diminished. I had apprehended and processed countless men and women for deportation, many of whom I sent without thinking to pass through this very room—but there was something dreadfully altered in their presence here between towering and cavernous walls, lorded over by foreign men in colored suits and black robes, men with little notion of the dark desert nights or the hard glare of the sun, with little sense for the sweeping expanses of stone and shale, the foot-packed earthen trails, the bodies laid bare before the elements, the bones trembling from heat, from cold, from want of water. It dawned on me that in my countless encounters with migrants at the hard end of their road through the desert, there was always the closeness of the failed journey, the fading but still-hot spark from the last flame of the crossing. But here, in the stale and swirling air of the courthouse, it was clear that something vital had gone missing in the days since apprehension, some final essence of the spirit had been stamped out or lost in the slow crush of confinement.

The pastor leaned forward and pointed toward a gray-haired man who had just stood to walk to the front of the courtroom. It's your dad, he whispered to the boys. They looked at the man and then at each other, wide-eyed. Es él, the pastor said, gesturing again and again, es él. The boys sat forward in their seats to get closer. No está, the boys confirmed with each other, no, no está. Yes, the pastor said emphatically, that's your father. You don't recognize him because he shaves his head, but his hair has grown out and he has stubble now, you can even see his bald spot. Se ve diferente. The boys looked at each other. Él es, Lupe said finally. It's him. The boys sat on their hands, dumbstruck, their mouths agape. Beside me, Lupe slowly doubled over, placing her forearms on her thighs with her palms open at the knees, her head sinking into her hands as she gently rocked in place, cradling herself in her own embrace.

As José shuffled through a row of chairs, the soft tinkling of his shackles seemed to fill the room. When I finally caught a glimpse of his profile, I saw the face of a man adrift at sea, his eyes scanning the horizon as if out of habit, with little actual hope of sighting land.

He wore a sweat-stained T-shirt that seemed to swallow him, and his body appeared small and gaunt and slumped inward, his face and head leathered and speckled with gray hair. As he turned, he caught sight of his three sons with their mouths open and their arms draped around their mother, who had finally lifted her head. He gasped audibly, his eyes dilating in disbelief. He looked away and then back again, focusing and unfocusing his vision in confirmation. Quiet sobs began to seize his children, and I wondered if I had done something terrible by bringing them here. José took one last look at his family, his mouth slack and twisted, his eyes wide with longing, and then, with great force, he began to thrash his head downward, to and fro, as if trying to shake a nightmare upon waking.

I'VE BEEN THINKING A LOT ABOUT THIS CASE, JOSÉ'S COURT-appointed attorney told me when we met a week after the Streamline hearing, in an empty hallway outside the courtroom. Alone among the forty or so others, who were convicted and sentenced without distinction, José had been granted a continuance at the request of his attorney and scheduled for a follow-up hearing. Walter, the attorney, had advised Lupe not to come—it's too risky to show up at the courthouse without papers, he told her. But the boys could come, he said, they're citizens, no problem. And so Lupe took the boys out of school once again to see their father in shackles and asked me if I would bring them. Of course, I said.

You know, Walter continued, I woke up thinking about Mr. Martínez in the middle of the night. It's not that his situation is unique, because it's not. But it's unusual to see so much support for someone in the courtroom, to see their family right there in the gallery. Walter was silent for several seconds. I have a son, he said, gesturing toward José's oldest—they're the same age. I woke up this morning and I could hear my son out in the kitchen. It got me thinking. No father should be kept from his family this way, no father should have a young son and wake up unable to hear him in the next room.

As I sat listening to Walter on a dark wooden bench, José's boys chased one another down the empty hallway and I wondered how the wide corridors of the courthouse must seem to them as they slid across the waxed floors. Watching them, I realized that I had little understanding of the place myself. I thought of the countless documents I had filled out during my years in the Border Patrol—voluntary return papers, expedited removal forms, reinstatements of prior deportation orders—documents sorted through by clerks and attorneys and judges, documents that followed the accused as they were shuttled across the state from one holding cell to the next. I realized, too, that despite my small role within the system, despite hours of training and studying at the academy, I had little inkling of what happened to those I arrested after I turned over their paperwork and went home from my shift.

For several minutes, Walter and I sat next to each other in silence. My mind had filled with questions, but I was wary of seeming too curious, wary that Walter might sense my old allegiance to the agency that was so often positioned against him. I asked sheepishly if he could explain to me why he had asked for the continuance. He thought about how best to explain. Well, he began, I'll start with the basics. There's criminal law and civil law, you probably know that. Charges related to illegal border crossing are criminal charges—so last week's hearing and this week's follow-up are both criminal proceedings. But citizenship and immigration fall under the umbrella of civil law. I nodded, remembering my tests at the academy. Walter went on. You've got to understand that most undocumented border crossers don't have any claim to citizenship or immigration status. But José's got family here, his kids are citizens. That's why I interjected during the Streamline hearing last week and asked the judge to delay José's sentencing. I hoped a continuance would give him some time to find an actual immigration lawyer, to see if they can put together a claim to be heard in civil court. They found someone, I said, the owner of the mercado is friends with a good lawyer. That's lucky, he said. Who is it? Elizabeth Green, I told him. Well, he replied, that's very lucky. Elizabeth has a great reputation. He glanced down the hallway at Vicente, José's youngest boy. I think she just had a baby, he added.

Walter turned back to me. I'll tell you what's going to happen today, he said. Mr. Martínez will still have to plead guilty to the misdemeanor crime of illegal entry, like everyone you saw last week. In turn, the government will offer him the same deal as before—dismissing the felony charge of reentry and sentencing him to thirty days in prison. Then, boom, José is done with the criminal charges. That's when things change. Instead of being immediately deported after fulfilling his sentence, José will then get kicked over into an immigration proceeding—the civil case. Elizabeth will be the one handling all that. The family will meet with her in the meantime and they'll put together an argument. I don't know much about the intricacies of immigration law, except that it's not free. You don't get a public defender like me. You gotta pay to play.

Walter gazed down the hallway at José's boys. You know, he said, it's difficult to see a man's life torn apart. A lot of people in the immigration system lose sight of people's humanity. I see it every day here. He gestured at the air all around him. The Border Patrol agents, the marshals I see here day in and day out, they objectify these people all the time. I clenched my jaw, not wanting to reveal myself.

I know a guy who works here, I told him. Oh yeah? he asked. What's his name? Morales. Shit, Walter said, I know Morales. He paused. I don't want to say anything bad about your buddy, but that Morales is a very serious guy. He's always seemed a bit callous to me. Yanking on people, pushing their chairs around, stuff like that. I looked at Walter and held my tongue.

You know, he said, as a public defender I've represented all sorts of people. I've even represented Border Patrol agents. One of my clients was framed by his own colleagues in the patrol because he was too human, because he showed too much compassion in the line of duty. The other agents didn't like him because he didn't play along with them, you know? He carried an injured woman on his back through the desert and the other agents started thinking he was soft, they didn't trust him, didn't like working with him, so they set the guy up. They framed him for brutality. They made it look like he had beaten someone up in the field. Isn't that twisted? I nodded. I tell you, Walter said, the Border Patrol, the marshals, it's like they forget about kindness. I've almost never seen these guys express any humanity, any emotion. I don't know how they do it. How do you come home to your kids at night when you spend your day treating other humans like dogs?

JOSÉ, DRESSED IN BRIGHT PRISONER ORANGE, LISTENED intently through a headset as the judge spoke to him.

I understand that you intend to plead guilty to the petty offense of illegal entry at a place other than one designated for entry by U.S. Immigration. In exchange for your plea, the government has agreed to dismiss the felony offense of reentry after removal.

This time José was the lone defendant in a modest-sized courtroom with few other occupants. Walter sat next to him and along the wall sat two U.S. marshals, both in dark suits, one of them tall with an angry pockmarked face, his gaze alternating intently between José and his boys. In a booth beside the judge's bench, a dark-skinned interpreter spoke hushed Spanish into a headset.

You must understand, the judge continued, that in the future this charge will always be used against you, that if you are arrested attempting to reenter the country, you could serve years in prison, not days or months. Next to me, José Junior drew a stick figure on the outside of an envelope. Look, he whispered to me, it's my brother.

Mr. Martínez, said the judge, are you a citizen of Mexico? Sí. On or about September 1, 2015, did you enter the United States near Yuma, Arizona? Sí. Did you come through a designated port of entry? No, señor. How do you plead in the charge of illegal entry? Culpable, señor.

AFTER THE HEARING, WALTER AND I SAT AGAIN ON A LONG bench outside the courtroom while the boys loped around the hallway, then disappeared. The sounds of their hollow yelling echoed out from the bathroom. You know, Walter told me, if Mr. Martínez hadn't left the country to see his dying mother, he would have been protected by the executive orders issued by President Obama. The orders granted provisional status and deferred deportation to noncriminal parents of U.S. citizens. José would have been home free. At the end of the hallway José's boys became visible again and I called out to Diego, the oldest. The other boys followed, pushing and circling each other behind him. What's with the yelling in the bathroom? I asked. I don't know, Diego said, we were just yelling. Because of the echo.

Suddenly, the doors to the courtroom opened in front of us and the tall man with the pockmarked face came striding out. He walked slowly over to the boys, now sitting at the far end of the bench. He stood craning over them and looked each of them in the face. Was that your dad in there? he asked. Yeah, Diego said meekly. Well, the man said, pausing for a moment—I'm sorry about your dad. Sometimes I feel pretty bad for you guys. He peered down at his chest and unfastened a small lapel pin with his massive hands. He grasped the pin in his fingers and stretched his arm out to Diego like a pilot offering his wings to a small boy. Diego took the pin and the man turned and walked back into the courtroom as Diego contemplated the object in his palm.

That's interesting, said Walter. I see that man in here all the time. I've never once seen him express any emotion. He shook his head. That's the first attempt at kindness I've ever witnessed here. I raised my eyebrows at him. Some people have more compassion than they let on, I told him.

Later, as I left the courtroom with the boys, I asked Diego if I could see the pin. He continued walking forward without stopping. Show it to him, said José Junior, the middle brother. He nudged Diego's shoulder. Reluctantly, Diego reached into his pocket. He clutched the pin in his fist, as if it had become something precious to him, then dropped it into my hand. The pin was heavy, made of real brass. It was a small star ringed by the words "United States Marshal." A tiny badge.

GROWING UP, MY MOTHER TELLS ME, SHE ALWAYS FELT ashamed to be Mexican. Her midwestern mother came from German and Irish roots, and her parents separated before she could form any memory of her father. Her mother, despite having fallen in love with a Mexican man, despite living in southwestern towns rich with Mexican heritage, despite being surrounded by Mexican coworkers and neighbors, nevertheless carried with her a certain attitude about Mexicans. As a child, my mother was told that she was messy, that she lied, that she was lazy, all because she was Mexican. If she found herself moved by ambition, if she felt driven by a sense of purpose, she was told it was her Irish work ethic, her exacting German focus. Even as she grew older, she found herself filled with shame whenever she procrastinated, whenever she felt the urge to put things off, as if she were battling an insidious and inferior lineage within.

Her mother had given her a single picture of her father. In the picture he was young and handsome, his face turned sideways to the camera, his eyes dark and squinting as he stared into the distance. He wore the traditional dress of a Mexican charro with a broad sombrero and a moño tied loosely around his neck. He held his left hand in front of his chin with his palm turned toward the sky and a cigarette hanging between his curled forefingers, a cone of ash ready to fall from the tip.

My mother would stare at this photo and swell with love for her father, imagining him as adventurous and dashing, mysterious and strong. She fantasized about meeting him. Finally, the summer she turned seventeen, she drove to his home in San Diego. She wore her most expensive shoes and her finest Mexican dress, white and brown gingham frilled with dark lace. Standing on his doorstep, she could hardly contain herself. Her father was a legend. She knocked at the door and waited to be greeted by a tall and elegantly dressed caballero. When the door finally opened, she beheld a short man in a white T-shirt, bald and grinning, a soft belly protruding from well-worn pleated pants.

My young mother came to find that her father was a man bound by family and tradition, a man who lived mere miles from his brothers and sisters, who spent his days indoors sorting mail for the postal service, who rarely ventured far from home, a man who, as she saw it, never took any risks. She found herself, after years of anticipation, ashamed of her father—ashamed, still, to be Mexican.

It wasn't until later, as a young adult, living and working in national parks, that she saw how a tradition of staying could serve to root people in a culture, to anchor them in a landscape. In the Great Smoky Mountains of Tennessee, in the farms and ranches of West Texas, in the canyonlands of the Colorado plateau, she saw how people loved and were shaped by the land. Finally, she traveled to the Coronado National Memorial on the border of Arizona and Sonora. She became friends with the superintendent of the park, a Mexican man proud of his heritage, born a citizen of both nations. For years he had worked in Mexico as a school principal. But in the Coronado Memorial, a place that marked the passage of Francisco Vásquez de Coronado across the lands that would come to hold a torrid boundary line—a place that commemorated the inception of a violent and unceasing exchange of cultures—he saw a place of international significance, a place that told his story.

My mother soon confided in the man, and he became the first

person she ever told about her lifelong shame of being Mexican. The man smiled at her. That's how it works, he told her. The first generation struggles to leave, to come into a new country, to gain acceptance in a new culture. Often they arrive and find themselves ostracized, they settle in pockets, they do everything they can just to get a toehold. Whether or not they learn English themselves, they know that their children must speak it. Sometimes they go so far as to discourage their children from speaking their own language— they want them to get into good schools, to identify with their new culture, to be accepted by it in all the ways they were not. The man looked knowingly at my mother as he explained. This second generation, he continued, might find themselves at great distance from the culture of their parents. Perhaps somewhere along the way they are told to put the old culture behind them, and so they find it within themselves to reject it.

As the second generation forms their own identity, he went on, it is more often built within the new culture rather than the old. By the time they have their own children, it usually turns out that this third generation is almost totally accepted. They have it easy—the culture of their grandparents' adopted country defines them wholly. However, he added, when they arrive at adulthood, they often begin to look around for something that makes them unique. And it's then that they begin to search for an inheritance, to look back for the traditions that make them special, and often they realize it isn't there. They realize something has been lost along the way.

My mother tells me that when I was born, she remembered the

words of this man, she remembered all the ways she had grown up alienated from her own identity. I didn't want that for my son, she tells me. I wanted you to feel pride, to find strength in your heritage.

OUTSIDE THE LAW OFFICES OF ELIZABETH GREEN, I SAT IN my truck, wondering what I was doing, what role I was playing, what protocols I had followed to arrive there. I sat with the engine idling, slowly shaking my head as I listened to the radio. It's simple, I finally told myself. This is what friends do.

Inside, a receptionist directed me to a conference room upstairs. I entered to find Elizabeth and Diane already seated across the table from each other, chatting about Elizabeth's newborn. I greeted Diane and introduced myself to Elizabeth. I work for Diane, I told her, I'm a friend of José's. Diane leaned over to Elizabeth. He can speak Spanish, she said. He's been a big help to the family. How nice, Elizabeth said. I took a seat near the end of the table beside a long window overlooking the mountains to the west. I listened to the women and eyed the clock. Lupe was late. It's hard to sleep at night, Elizabeth was telling Diane, I hear him crying out for me in the next room. It's almost like I can hear him breathing through the walls.

My phone rang. Lupe had arrived and needed help finding the office. I excused myself to go outside. In the parking lot I found her walking with the pastor. I greeted them both. Nice to see you again, I told the pastor, how good of you to come.

Upstairs Elizabeth greeted everyone and invited us to sit down.

She began in Spanish, speaking directly to Lupe in slow, deliberate sentences. Unfortunately, she said, José's situation is not rare. She looked around the room. But it is rare to see so many people here for one case. Usually only the immediate family comes to a meeting like this. Elizabeth looked at Lupe and then gestured at me, Diane, and the pastor. José must have made quite an impression on you all, she said. Lupe watched us with her hands gathered in her lap. Elizabeth went on. I want to talk with you today about José so we can find the best strategy to keep him here. We are going to do everything we can, she told Lupe. Elizabeth placed a hand on the table and repeated her words. Todo lo posible.

Elizabeth switched into English and glanced at me. Do you mind translating? she asked. No, I said, of course not. I want to make a few things clear, she began, I want to temper expectations right off the bat. This case is going to be hard, not impossible, but hard. She looked across the table at Diane. I also want to be clear that even if José is able to stay, it is unlikely that he'll be able to come back to work for you, because at this point, of course, you are no longer ignorant of his undocumented status. Diane shook her head. It's a shame—José was such a great employee, such a sweet man. Well, Elizabeth said, it's rare to see an employer invested in someone enough to come to these meetings, rare for them to support someone's case against deportation. Diane shrugged. I really thought he had everything in order, she said. At first we hired him on as an independent contractor. He filled out all his paperwork, had a social security number, and at the end of each year we gave him a 1099. It never occurred to me that even after months and years of working with us he never asked to be put on payroll, never asked for benefits. Maybe he wanted to keep things vague to protect himself, to protect us from knowing his status. Diane looked around the table. I just never thought about it.

Elizabeth leaned on the table. Given what you knew, she said to Diane, there's legally nothing wrong with what you did. But I want you to know that even in the best-case scenario, José has no chance of being granted legal status. I want to be clear here, to you, but most of all to Lupe, that what we are asking for in this case is not legalization. Under existing law, José doesn't really have a path to legal status until his oldest son turns eighteen and can sponsor his mother and father for citizenship. And because José has a prior deportation on his record from 1996, we don't have a lot of options.

Elizabeth turned to Lupe. I want to ask you a few questions to start off, she said. She glanced at me and I began to translate. First of all, besides his past deportation, has José ever been in trouble with the law? Lupe shook her head. No, she said, never. She looked over at the pastor. José used to drink, she admitted quietly. The pastor bowed his head. But he never got into any trouble, Lupe said, gracias a Dios. Ever since our first son was born he hasn't had a single drink. Good, Elizabeth said. This next question might be hard for you to answer, she continued, but it's an important one. Have you, José, or the boys ever been the victims of a violent crime here in the U.S.? Lupe looked down at her hands still clasped in her lap. No, she said. La verdad es que no.

So, Elizabeth concluded, that leaves us with two options. The first is for José to claim fear of returning to Mexico. In that case he would be held for a screening interview to see if he is eligible for something like asylum. He would remain in immigration custody for at least six months prior to being released on bond.

I'm sorry, Lupe said, what does that mean exactly? She looked at Elizabeth. Fear of returning to Mexico? Of course he has fear. La violencia, she said, la delincuencia, la corrupción. Elizabeth began to tap a pencil against her legal pad. Of course, she said, I'm sorry. What I mean by fear is something more specific. If José has received death threats, for example, from a drug cartel or some other group. If he's part of an ethnic or political minority that is being targeted somewhere. Land disputes, blood feuds between or among families, things like this.

Lupe clutched her hands in her lap and looked down, shaking her head. No, she said, nothing like that. Elizabeth rested her pencil at the top of her pad. Well, she said, I'll visit José in the detention center and talk with him just to be sure. But to be clear, the ultimate goal of an asylum application wouldn't really be to win. Almost no one wins asylum from Mexico, only about one percent of Mexican cases are actually granted asylum. But the process buys time, and the application would bolster a request for a stay of removal. As I translated Elizabeth's words Lupe stared at me, expressionless.

So, Elizabeth went on, that brings us to our second option, which is to ask for a deferred deportation under the executive actions that, for the time being, protect certain undocumented immigrants such as noncriminal parents of U.S. citizens. The problem, of course, is that José has a prior deportation from 1996, and on top of that, his most recent exit and illegal reentry into the country. That means he's now considered a "recent entrant," and recent entrants are a priority for deportation even under these executive actions. So what we need to do is try to make a great case for prosecutorial discretion. Basically, that means we would present to a judge all the compelling reasons that José should still be granted a stay of removal despite his recent entry. The goal here is to get José out of detention and, essentially, to buy time with the appeals process and hope for better policy and eventual immigration reform down the line. José would still have no work permit, he'd still be living in the shadows, but he'd be protected, he could remain there safely, if that makes any sense.

Elizabeth shifted her gaze around the room, looking in turn at Diane, Lupe, the pastor, and me. So, she began again, here's what I will need from all of you: From you, Lupe, any and all documentation that establishes how long José has lived and worked in the States. Pay stubs and any tax information that proves employment, rental or lease agreements, utility contracts, anything else that establishes proof of continual residence. How long has José been in the U.S.? Lupe thought for a moment. More than thirty years, she answered.

Elizabeth seemed surprised. Well, she said, if you can produce documents that establish a continual presence here for more than thirty years, that will be very good for his application. Also, she continued, we'll need any legal documents you can produce regarding your children: birth certificates, report cards, health records. Health records are important. Do your boys have any health issues? Lupe looked toward her pastor and then over at me. My youngest son Vicente has a problem with his brain. He has problems speaking. She looked down at the floor. José Junior has asthma. He was hit by a car, too, she said, a year and a half ago. He still has a limp. And Diego, my oldest, had meningitis. I'm sorry to hear that, Elizabeth told her. Documentation of all of this will be very important for the application—any evidence you can give of their medical conditions will help the case.

Elizabeth turned toward me, Diane, and the pastor. Another thing that will help José's case are testimonies to his good character, she said. Letters from current and past employers, landlords, neighbors, churchgoers, and family members, particularly those with legal status. The more the better. Any evidence of community service he's taken part in as a church member or in any other capacity would also help. The author should be sure to state how many years they've known José, in what capacity they've known him, and why they support him—moral character, work ethic, et cetera. Examples are good, and the author should list specific things José has done that have impressed them or demonstrated that José is someone special or unique. If the author is familiar with the hardships his removal would place upon the family, that should be included in the letter as well. As Elizabeth spoke I gazed out the window to the mountains, wondering how such hardships could be put into words.

There's one last thing I'll need to get started, Elizabeth stated, and that's half the money to pay for our legal fees. Two thousand dollars of the four thousand total. We'll pay for half, Diane said, my husband and I have already decided. Lupe's eyes widened, catching the glare from the sunlight filtering in through the windows. The pastor leaned forward in his chair and placed his arms on the table. The church will help Lupe to pay the other half, he said. Elizabeth smiled. Fantastic, she said. Lupe looked around the room, unsure of what to say or how to react.

Are there any questions? Elizabeth asked us. Diane held her hand up near her face. Maybe it's a bad time to ask, she said, but what happens if José's case is denied? Well, Elizabeth said, he'll be sent back to Mexico, of course, and that will happen quickly, right after the deportation order is issued. Sometimes we don't find out until after the decision has been made, after the person has already been deported. Immigration decisions don't happen in a courtroom, so we won't be arguing our case before a judge. We submit the documents and the decision is made behind closed doors.

If José is deported, the charge will appear on his record, of course, and that will make it harder for him when and if he tries to legalize down the line. With this deportation he'll receive a five-year ban on reentry. Diane sighed. And if he tries to cross again? she asked. Elizabeth picked up her pencil. He'll serve more jail time each time he's picked up, she said. Instead of thirty days, next time it will probably be sixty, then ninety. And he'll be banned from reentry for ten years, then twenty, and so on.

Elizabeth looked at Lupe and then eyed me to make sure I was ready to translate again. I want to be sure that you know where your husband is, she said. He'll be at the state detention center for the duration of the thirty-day sentence he was issued at the criminal hearing. Lupe nodded at me and then at Elizabeth. After that, Elizabeth said, if José's case is still under consideration, which it probably will be, he'll be placed in the nearby immigration detention center. Elizabeth scrawled a number on a piece of paper and handed it to Lupe. This is his inmate number, she said, you'll need it if you have any dealings with the prison. Elizabeth tapped the pencil against her legal pad. Do you have questions? she asked. Just one, Lupe said. Can the boys see their father? Elizabeth sat back in her chair. Well, she said, yes—the detention center allows visitation. She rested her pencil back on the table. But they check papers there, so it wouldn't be safe for you to go. You'd have to find someone else to take the boys.

I DROVE THROUGH THE TRAILER PARK IN THE EARLY MORNING, before the sun was up, looking for José's home. I finally found it—a doublewide with two doors in a dirt lot next to a dumpster. The lights were off and I knocked at each of the doors. After several minutes of waiting I knocked louder until I finally heard rustling inside and saw a light come on. Lupe opened the door and smiled weakly, her face heavy with sleep. Diego's getting ready, she said, he'll be out in a few minutes. Is it just him? I asked. Yes, she said, the little ones should rest.

In the car Diego was silent. Did you already eat? I asked. Not really, he said. We stopped at a McDonald's and I ordered a sausage McMuffin and Diego ordered two sausage breakfast burritos. As we waited to pull up to the window, he handed me money. It's okay, I told him, I'll pay. No, he said, my mom gave me this money. She'd be mad if you paid. Okay, I told him, okay. I smiled. Thanks for breakfast.

You know, I said as he unwrapped his first burrito, your dad used to eat a breakfast burrito every morning at work. He would always give me half. I stared out at the road and took a bite of my sandwich. I asked Diego about school, about what he did for fun. I like soccer, he said. Oh, yeah? I asked. What's your favorite club? I don't really have one, he said, I just like to play. I play in the park with my brothers. My dad used to take us. I'm on a team from church too. He took another bite from his burrito. What position do you play? I asked. I'm a striker, he said, I'm the one that makes the goals.

After nearly an hour of driving, the sun finally rose above the horizon and cast its first rays upon the desert flatlands and fields dormant with crops. We slowed as we began to pass buildings and houses and we soon made out the prison complexes towering in the distance. We drove through quiet streets past a high school, a trading post, an Italian restaurant, until we finally arrived at the massive detention center at the opposite edge of town. Outside, a guard in a white truck was checking vehicles at the entrance to the parking lot. I rolled down my window. We're here for visitation, I told him. What cell block? I read him the information I had taken down. That block doesn't have visitation until nine, he said. Really? I asked. But online it said— The guard cut me off. Nine a.m., he repeated. I looked at Diego and then back at the guard. Is there somewhere we can wait? I asked. I could feel him glaring at me through his sunglasses. There's a diner in town, he said. You can wait there.

It was nearly seven when we pulled into the diner parking lot. Diego and I sat in a booth by the window and stared out in silence as the amber light of the sun spilled across the asphalt. A waitress sauntered over with two menus and a pitcher of water. Good morning, she said, I'll bet you boys are hungry. I looked up at her and smiled. To tell you the truth, I said, we already ate. We're waiting for visitation at the prison. You must get that a lot. Sometimes, she said. Well, I continued, is it all right if we nurse some coffee and order something small? She smiled and nodded toward the only other customer, a stout man in a cowboy hat bantering at the counter with another waitress. Any business is good business, she said.

The waitress took our menus and left and we stared again out the window. Do your parents let you drink coffee? I asked Diego. Yeah, he said, but I don't really like how it tastes. Your dad drinks it with vanilla and cream, I told him. I turned my head and looked across the table at him, small and slumped against the back of the booth. Oh, he said. I didn't know. I never saw my dad in the mornings.

Two hours later, back at the entrance to the prison, the guard in the white truck stuck his hand out the window as we approached. I rolled down the window. Visitation is closed. It's nine a.m., I said, what do you mean? There's a riot in cell block E. Visitation is closed. I looked at Diego and then back at the guard. For how long? I asked. The man shrugged. How am I supposed to know? Until they stop rioting.

I ARRANGED TO MEET LUPE IN THE MERCADO AT THE END OF my shift. I had offered to help her sort through documents and deliver them to Elizabeth's law firm. She was seated at a small table with her hair pulled back in a tight bun. She smiled as I approached, standing to greet me with timid familiarity. As we sat down, she slung a large woven bag into her lap and pulled out a thick stack of papers loosely gathered in a manila folder. I briefly scanned through them. There were documents from 1981, from 1990, from 1993, 1994, 1997, 2002, 2003, 2005, 2009, 2012, 2015, there were José's old ID cards, pay stubs and W-2s, insurance forms, rental agreements, utility bills, medical records, statements of payment and credit history—everything stacked together in no particular order, a bulging dossier on a life lived at the workaday margins of a country now set in motion against him.

I left the documents with Lupe and asked her to excuse me for a minute. I walked across the courtyard and knocked on the open door to Diane's office. Come in, I heard her say. Lupe's here, I said, and she's got a lot of documents. Good, Diane replied. Actually, I said, they're kind of a mess. Is there a big table somewhere where we can lay them out and organize things? Of course. Diane led me down the hall to a conference room. It's free until later this afternoon, she told me. Do you need anything else? Maybe some markers and a set of folders, I said. There's office supplies in the next room, she offered. Take whatever you need.

For the next two hours, Lupe and I stood at the conference table sorting through piles of papers, some of them faded and yellowing: documents providing evidence of José's entry into the United States at age eleven and the work he had been engaged in every year thereafter, earning minimum wage as a dishwasher, a busboy, a custodian, an auto repairman, a maintenance man, a farmworker, a fruit picker, an agricultural equipment operator, a carpet mill factory worker, a truck driver, a construction hand; documents providing certification of his marriage, certification of the birth of each of his three sons, certification of his mother's death; documents providing evidence of the growing lives of his children, children who visited the school nurse and the local health clinic, children who received brain scans, behavioral health reports, cognitive speech and language therapy, children who received report cards and teacher's notes, children who were being shaped by the twin identities of immigrant and citizen.

As Lupe and I sorted through the documents, I labeled distinct folders and placed each document in its corresponding place. WORK, I scrawled on one folder, RESIDENCE on another. I labeled one folder DEPENDENTS and placed a folder for each child inside it, and within each of these, separate folders labeled SCHOOL, MEDICAL, and PROOF OF CITIZENSHIP. I saw ID photos of José as a young man with feathered black hair, his skin dark and glaring with the light from the flashbulb. I saw ID photos of his sons, their faces round with baby fat, and I saw the prints of their newborn hands and feet inked on the hospital documents that certified their birth. I saw his and Lupe's signatures, over and over again, printed simply in block letters on form after form, year after year.

When we finally finished, I walked with Lupe back across the courtyard. As we said our goodbyes, a woman named Ana, a worker at the Mexican bakery, stepped into the courtyard to greet Lupe. She asked about José, about the boys, about the stack of documents in my hands. They're for José's case, Lupe said, he's taking them to the lawyer. Ana smiled at me. It's so nice of you to help the family, she said. She touched me on the shoulder and looked at Lupe, lowering her voice. It's hard to imagine that he was la migra, isn't it? Oh really? Lupe asked, her eyes widening in surprise. José didn't tell you? No, she said, elongating the word. That's right, continued Ana—he saw what we go through at the border, and look, now he's helping. I smiled and nodded, wondering if that's what this really was, if I was merely being driven to make good for the lives I had sent back across the line, if I was seeking to dole out some paltry reparation. If I was seeking redemption, I wondered, what would redemption look like?

LUPE CAME TO THE DOOR AFTER MY FIRST KNOCK. GOOD morning. She smiled. It's not so early this time, she said. She disappeared into the house and I could hear her calling after Diego.

She came back to the door with papers in her hand. Disculpa, she said, but would you mind if José Junior came too? Last time he was so sad not to go. Cómo no, I said. I gestured at the documents in her hand. Are those his papers? Yes, she said, handing them over. Diego walked up behind his mother and stood beside her in the doorway. You're almost as tall as your mom, I said. He stood up straight and smiled. Actually, he said, I'm taller. His mother swiped at him playfully. I'm almost as tall as my dad, he said proudly.

As we drove north toward the detention center, Diego looked at his phone and José Junior played a game of soccer on an iPod Touch in the backseat, pumping his hand in the air each time he scored a goal and then passing the device up to his brother, insisting he watch each computer-generated replay. After about ten minutes, Diego became bored with his phone and turned around in his seat. Let me play, he said to José Junior. But you have your phone, his brother whined. I know, Diego replied, but it doesn't have soccer.

José Junior surrendered the iPod and looked around the inside of the vehicle. I hope we get back before school's out, he said. I turned and looked at him. He was clutching the shoulder strap of his seat belt. Why? I thought most kids loved to skip school. Not me, he said. I like school. Yesterday my teacher said she was going to give us treats at the end of the day today. We even voted on what kind of cupcakes we like. Diego thrust his arm up in the seat next to me. GOL! he shouted. He turned to his brother. Look, Diego said, showing his brother the replay—I'm going to score a goal just like this on Saturday.

After several minutes, José Junior leaned toward Diego from the backseat and touched him on the shoulder. Look, he said, it's floating. Diego put down the iPod. What are you talking about? That thing on the side of the road, José Junior said, if you stare at it, it looks like it's floating. Diego looked out his window at the passing road. I don't get it, he said, what do you mean? The bar, José Junior said. I turned and looked out the window at the guardrail running along the shoulder of the highway. When I stared at it straight on, the wooden posts holding it up blurred together as they sped past, giving the illusion of a steel barrier hovering above the ground. You mean the guardrail? I asked. José Junior smiled at me. Yeah, he said. It's floating.

At the detention center I reminded the boys to leave everything in the car. Phones, iPods, wallets, even your belts, I said. We followed another visitor across the lot toward a gate in the towering two-tiered fence topped with coils of concertina wire. After five of us had gathered in front of the gate, it slowly wheeled open by remote and we passed through into the sally port, waiting patiently for it to close again behind us. Above me, I heard the call of a mourning dove lilting up from somewhere on the roof of the prison. The wind blew gently against the wires, jostling the arms of a bumpy and bare-skinned cactus beside the walkway. José Junior nudged Diego. It sounds like our mom is talking to us. I looked at the chain-link fence trembling with the gusts of cool air. You mean the wind, I asked him, or the birds? José Junior thought for a second. All of it, he said.

José Junior held his hand up to his face to block the sun and looked toward the door of the prison. I feel like I've been here before, he said to me. Really? I asked. Yeah, like maybe in a dream. He walked to the cactus at the end of the walkway and I noticed, for the first time, a slight limp in his gait. He looked up at the fence, and his baggy T-shirt, a hand-me-down from one of his brothers, rippled in the wind.

The gate finally closed behind us with a metallic crash and a guard opened the door to the prison. I watched the two women in front of us make their way through the line. Following their example, I took a sheet of paper from a countertop and filled out José's name, inmate number, and cell block. When it was my turn at the window I handed the paper to the guard. He typed at his computer and chewed at a bushy white mustache. Martínez-Cruz? he finally asked. Yes sir, I said. What's your relation? I'm a friend, I replied, and these are his boys. Are you their guardian? For the day, I said. I handed him a notarized letter from Lupe. Do you have their papers? he asked. Yes sir, I said, handing him the boys' birth certificates. The man typed some more and then instructed us to empty our pockets and pass through the metal detector into the waiting room.

The boys sat next to one another in hard plastic seats. Diego fidgeted with his hands and José Junior swung his legs back and forth. The two women who came in before us sat across from each other in facing chairs. I like your shoes, one woman said to the other, are they Vans? Coach, she answered. Oh. The woman looked down at her legs and wiggled her feet. I just got these at Dollar

General. That works too, the other woman said. They're kind of cute. After a few more minutes, the woman with Coach shoes asked the other if she had visited the prison before. One other time, the woman answered, on a Sunday. It was busy, she said, shaking her head. I think weekdays are the way to go. I looked back at the boys. José Junior sat holding his face in his hands.

To pass the time I began to walk around the room, gazing at the posters on the wall from the Corrections Corporation of America. "Zero Tolerance Suicide Prevention," said one, "Be a hero, keep it at zero." "Opportunity is knocking," said another, "CCA is currently accepting applications." Another poster depicted a smiling black man: "I believe everybody needs a little fun in their life. I am Terry Williams Jr., a Senior Corrections Officer in Tennessee. I am CCA." Next to it, another showed an older white woman beaming with pride: "My name is Mary Bowermaster. I am a shift supervisor in Florida and I believe you should never stop learning. I am CCA." And another: "I get to teach people how to live better lives. I am Jason Russel, a nurse and a woodworker in Mississippi. I am CCA." I stood before the photographed faces and thought about the kinship I shared with them—the badge, the gun, the wrangling of human beings, the slow severing of spirit. In the distance, jangling keys began to echo through the room and I turned my head to hear the calling of the guards.

We were given sheets of paper and instructed to walk back to our cars and drive around the building to another entrance. I'm confused, I said to a guard, I thought this was visitation. This is check-in, the guard said, visitation is on the other side. Back in the car, I followed the woman with Coach shoes as she drove around the building to make sure I arrived at the right entrance. I ushered the boys out of the car once again and joined the two women in front of another entrance, where we waited for another gate to open. Diego shuffled his feet and José Junior stood looking again at the top of the fence. I really don't know why I have the feeling I've been here before, he said. He looked down at the ground. I can't handle the pressure, José Junior mumbled to himself. What do you mean? I asked. I don't know if I can handle talking to my dad. I looked to Diego and then back at his brother. Why not? José Junior sighed. Because he's in jail.

We were finally let in through the prison doors by the same mustachioed guard who had taken our documents at check-in. He took the sheets of paper we had been given and instructed us to pass once again through a metal detector. We were led down a hallway and made to wait for several minutes while the guard chatted with a coworker who had just finished his shift. I'll catch you in D block tomorrow, the guard said. Hell no you won't, his coworker replied, I've got the day off. I'm taking the wife and kids to the ballpark. Well, the guard scoffed, look at you.

The guard led us to a doorway and stopped to give us instructions before letting us through. You'll have forty-five minutes to visit, he said, and I'll give a ten-minute warning before time is up. You'll be using the phones mounted on the wall next to the window, he continued, each prisoner has a code to dial out. Wait until the phone rings before you pick it up or else you won't have a connection. Plastic chairs are stacked against the back wall to the right, grab one as you enter the room and stack them back where you got them on your way out. As the guard spoke, I noticed that he looked only at the women and me, that he never lowered his gaze to regard the boys.

When he opened the door I stood behind the boys and ushered them forward. The inside of the visitation room was brightly lit with cinderblock walls painted in pale tan. The two women were first through the door and walked directly to the stack of plastic chairs. The guard closed the door behind us and then walked to a desk in the corner of the room and took a seat behind a computer monitor. The boys stood unmoving just a few feet beyond the entrance, staring at their father as he waved from behind a reinforced glass window. He smiled widely at them, standing on his feet, swaying from side to side. I kneeled down to speak to the boys. Go ahead, I told them, I'll bring the chairs.

When I walked up to the window, José Junior had already taken up the receiver and was speaking with his father. José's head and face were shaved and he looked strong again, like he had regained the weight he'd lost in the desert. José Junior remained standing at the window even after I placed a chair behind him. He spoke eagerly with his father about school, about his friends at church. He told his father that he missed him, that it was sad at the house without him.

Behind us, the guard stood up from his computer and placed something in a microwave on a countertop next to the desk. The

beeping of the keypad rang out through the room and I watched
the man chew at his mustache as he stood waiting for his meal. On
either side of me, I observed the women speaking to men clad in
orange, their faces held close against the glass. This is love, one
woman said into the receiver. Things are the same out here, the
other woman said softly. Everything is the same.

I looked back at José and watched the way he tilted his head as he
gazed through the glass, the way he smiled as he listened to his son.
I watched the motion of his mouth, the way he spoke and laughed.
It was like watching a man on mute, I thought, a man who, despite
his proximity, would not be heard even if he was crying out on the
other side of the glass, even if he was screaming.

After ten minutes or so, José Junior handed the phone to Diego.
José smiled warmly as his oldest son told him about soccer, about
playing with his brothers in the park. His face grew more serious as
Diego spoke with him about his grades, about his youngest brother's
health, about what he was doing to help Lupe around the house. At
times José stared down at the ground, closing his eyes and rubbing
his brow. Mom is working a lot more, Diego told him, she gets annoyed with us sometimes. But she's fine, he said, she's just tired.

Diego set the phone down on the ledge beneath the window. My
dad wants to talk to you, he told me. Oh, I said. Sure. I stood and
grabbed my chair, moving it closer to the window. I picked up the
handset. Paco, José said to me, smiling. His voice sounded tinny
and distant in the receiver. I smiled back. José. Brother.

LUPE CAME BY THE COFFEE SHOP IN THE MORNING ON HER way back from dropping the boys at school and delivered a packet of letters she had collected from family, friends, neighbors, former employers, and fellow church members. I had arranged to deliver them to the law firm as soon as my shift was over. She handed me the envelope and smiled timidly. I noticed a tinge of apprehension in her gaze, as if she was still trying to comprehend the image of me as a lawman, trying to discern in me an old shadow of darkness. It's been so good of you to help us, she said. I shook my head. It's nothing. José is a friend. I looked away. Lupe glanced toward the door. I've got to get ready for work, she told me, I'm picking up shifts at the restaurant where José used to work. Qué bien, I said. Estamos en contacto. She waved goodbye and walked across the courtyard to her car.

At the end of my shift, I drove to Elizabeth's office and sat with my engine running in the parking lot. I opened the envelope that contained José's letters and began to flip through them. Some were typed, but most were handwritten, many of them in Spanish. They all began with some variation of "To Whom It May Concern." They referred to José as a brother in Christ, a family man, a good father, a responsible husband, a reliable person, always working hard, always giving his best, always offering to help with a smile on his face, always laughing.

To whom this may concern, began one letter: My name is Brenda

Collar, I have lived in the United States of America for over twenty-five years, and am now a proud US citizen. I have known my fellow friend and brother José for over three years approximately. We congregate at the same church and we both serve in the ushers department. José Martínez has always been such a joy to be around. He is a responsible and caring father which is projected from his three young sons. José Martínez is a hardworking man who has never left a task uncompleted. It would be a mistake to let such a hard worker, responsible father, and awesome friend go. Please consider my testimony and if there are further questions feel free to contact me.

Another man from José's church wrote: José is a good father, a good husband and a good employee. He is a good example of a good citizen. He always helps people instead of looking for help.

Many friends and family members made an effort to write their letters in a way that echoed the language of official documents: I, Leticia Martínez, declare under penalty of perjury that the following statement is true and correct to the best of my knowledge and recollection. To Whom It May Concern, I'm Leticia Martínez I'm José's niece he has been living in this country for many years, he is a very nice person he does not drink or smoke or use any drugs. He is a very responsible and hardworking person I wish that he had a chance to let him stay with his children in this country. Thanks for taking the time to read this letter.

To whom it may concern, wrote another man: In the matter of allowing José Martínez to stay in the United States of America. I

Pablo G. Martínez believe José M. should be allowed to stay in the country for the following reasons. He is a hardworking man that holds down two jobs. He is the head of household, without him his family would struggle very much both financially and emotionally. He has three little boys who need their father in their lives. He is one of the most respectable people I know and should definitely be allowed to stay in this great country.

Lupe wrote in Spanish on lined school paper borrowed from her children: I Lupe Balderas declare that José Martínez-Cruz is my husband since the year 1999. We have 3 boys age 15, 10, and 8. We were always a very exemplary family we would go out when my husband was off work. He was the only one who worked. He had two jobs and his free time was dedicated to us. My husband is an exemplary father and a caring spouse. He doesn't drink, he doesn't smoke, he doesn't use drugs he only dedicates himself to making his family happy but now we miss him very much because I Lupe cannot take my boys to the park because lately I have been unwell. My husband took my boys to play soccer every Wednesday and on weekends he dedicated his time to us to eat and go out and now we miss him. My husband has given sixteen years of happiness and love to my sons and me but we won't return to Mexico because my boys don't know anyone there and they speak very little Spanish and it's very difficult to adapt to another country when their whole life has been here they were born here and they are growing here. For us as parents we want the best for our sons Diego, José Junior, and Vicente. We miss my husband because he was responsible at home. I am his wife and I love him very much and I miss him. Diego, José Junior, and Vicente miss him. We love you very much we give hope to God that very soon we will be together because God does not like to see his children separated.

Vicente Martínez, José's youngest boy, wrote his own name at the top of a letter scrawled in pencil on ruled school paper. There were no spaces between his words, and his writing was riddled with misspellings and backward letters. Hi Daddy I love you because you take us to the park and to play soccer I miss you because you take us to the stores and you take us to go to work and to get money to feed us. The final two lines of Vicente's letter were incomprehensible, a jumble of letters that sometimes approximated words and sounds in Spanish. The Spanish word for God, Dios, could be discerned and, perhaps, the word for church, iglesia. I miss you very much, Vicente wrote clearly at the end, te extraño mucho.

José Junior had written on two half sheets of paper. On one of them he wrote a brief letter addressed to his father, much like that of his younger brother. At the bottom of the message he taped a wallet-sized picture of himself with tattered edges. On the second sheet of paper José Junior drew his family on a soccer field with frowning faces, the stick figures labeled MOM, BROTHER, BIG BROTHER. Below it was another drawing, almost identical, except this time the stick figures had smiles on their faces and an extra figure drawn next to them, labeled DAD.

Diego wrote a letter that continued across several sheets of paper. At two and a half pages, it was the longest of any in the packet. In its opening paragraphs, Diego seemed to realize that his father would likely not see or read his words, and he did his best to maintain a formal tone. Dear to who it may concern, the letter began, Hi I'm Diego Martínez I'm the son of José Martínez I'm his oldest son I am 15 years old. I have two younger brothers. One is 10 and the other is 8. I'm working to keep my brothers happy to buy them what they want to keep them happy. Well my dad José is the nicest guy I know my dad is like my best friend and my father. I treat my dad with so much respect he's the father any kid would want to have. My mom and my whole family broke down when we saw him at court on the first court he had everyone started crying. And the second court when his friend to work took me and my brothers. I broke down so much when I heard his voice it got me into so much tears. I miss my dad he knew how to cheer us up when we were down. He took us to the park on Monday and Wednesday to play soccer with our church friend he got along with everyone at church my dad was the coolest person most nicest, most religious, most caring person always made my mom happy, always putting a smile in our faces every single day he's also very smart and very funny. My dad always has a smile on his face trying to always help people who are in need. How I feel right now about my dad being in jail and seeing him like this makes me really sad depressed my father isn't here with us everyone that asks me about my dad makes me sad to say he's in jail. My heart kinda stops pauses and breaks down on every letter they send him he was a man with three children and one woman. Each one of my friends I've had for many years loved my dad because he took us to places like to any place appropriate, to mountains in the west to parks to many places in the city. My dad did anything to make us happy now my life is depressing hollow my dad's not here. A missing place for him here waits. My dad's a very responsible man. When I was little my dad was always by my side and always will still be by my side. I pray to God that my dad is always okay. I miss my dad so much it's really hard to express and write. I miss you so much dad. You always told us to never look back and always look forward thanks for always being there for us and never letting us go dad. We miss you so much. Just remember God is always by our side never letting us go. We all want them to set you free here. Everyone at church and his two works misses him a lot. Everyone misses my dad nobody wants him to get sent back to Mexico. Everyone's praying for you to let you out safely and still the same José we know. Dad we have a tournament for soccer for church on the twenty six of this month. I'll be making goals for you, the goals will be for you. You taught me how to play soccer and told me never to give up dad I'm a win that trophy for us. I'm training with everything I got to get better each day. Thank you to whoever got the time to read this I'm sorry it's so long it's because I really love my dad we all do and we're all sad to know he's in jail. Sincerely, his oldest son Diego Martínez.

AS I DROVE HOME AFTER A SHIFT AT THE COFFEE SHOP MY phone lit up with a text message: Hey its Diego I just wanted to tell u that their going to deport my dad back in the night.

Then, a few hours later, an email from Elizabeth Green: Unfortunately, I just received a message from the deportation officer that our request for prosecutorial discretion and a stay of removal was denied. I know no one wants this news. José had a great application with more support than I have seen in any of my other requests. They did not give a reason for the denial. The message states that José will be removed to Mexico this evening.

I stared at the screen, thinking of Lupe and the boys, wondering where José would sleep in the night.

In the evening I received a text message from Lupe: I'm sorry but can u call the lawyer José needs to see my baby because he fell and their going to operate. I called Lupe right away. Vicentito is in the hospital, she told me, he fell and broke his arm playing soccer in the park. They're going to put screws in his arm, she said. I told her that I was sorry, that I would help in any way I could. But why do you want me to call the lawyer? I asked. Oh, Lupe said hurriedly, so that José can come see Vicente before they send him back. She sounded desperate, at the edge, with something in her voice I had not yet heard. I tried to speak gently. There's no way to get ahold of José, I said. Immigration agents have him now, they're taking him back to the border. The lawyer can't contact them. Oh, I heard her say. I tried to come up with some words of comfort—I'm sure José will call when he's across the border, I said. Lupe was silent. Okay, she finally said. I understand.

AS I WALKED TREMBLING IN THE NIGHT THROUGH THE streets of my neighborhood, I called my mother. She asked how I was doing and I answered unthinkingly. I'm fine, I said. You don't sound fine, she finally said. What do you mean? I asked. My mother sighed. I'm your mother, she said, I can sense it. You've been distant. I felt an edge in her voice. This feels like it used to feel, she finally said. I stopped walking. I don't understand, I told her. It's like when you were on the border, she said. All those years I knew things were weighing on you, but you were so sensitive to my questions—I couldn't ask about it, I couldn't show concern, I could never reach you. I don't want that again. I'm too tired for it now.

I stood for a while at the side of the street, staring out at the houses of my neighbors. Finally, I sat down on the curb. When did you know? I asked. She paused. Something had gone away from our conversations, she said. I don't know how to describe it. She searched for a better explanation. There's a story I remember from Catholic school, she told me. There was this brilliant child, a music prodigy. He could play anything—he would hear birds sing and then turn it into music. At a very young age he was sent away to be trained by monks. When he arrived at the monastery they forbade him from hearing any music but his own, they forbade him from listening to any of the famous composers. They wanted him to write and create his own music, and for many years he did—he created the most phenomenal things. But as he got a bit older he became frustrated. He wanted to study, he wanted to hear other kinds of music. And so one day he snuck away from the monastery. He went to a nearby town and went into a concert hall, where he heard Mozart. When he came back, he didn't tell anyone, he kept creating new music just like before. A few days after his return, the monks heard him playing and they told him to stop. You've broken the rule, they told him. He looked at them with panic and insisted, no I haven't, I haven't, I haven't. They shook their heads and said, yes you have, you've discovered Mozart. No, he said, how could you know that? Because, they said, when you played without knowing, you played music from every composer—and now Mozart is missing.

When she finished the story, my mother fell silent. I sat hunched on the curb, the phone pressed against my ear. My friend, I finally told her, he's been deported. I felt unable to breathe. I fear for him, I said, I fear for his family. All these years, I told her, it's like I've been circling beneath a giant, my gaze fixed upon its foot resting at the ground. But now, I said, it's like I'm starting to crane my head upward, like I'm finally seeing the thing that crushes.

ON THE PHONE LUPE TOLD ME THAT JOSÉ WAS SAFE. HE'S staying at the border, she said, with a man from our church. He has food and shelter there. Gracias a Dios, she kept saying, bendito sea Dios. She told me that José hadn't decided his next move yet, but that he was looking for someone to cross him again. I wanted to tell her no, that José should not risk his life, that he should find some other way, but I knew, with sinking certainty, that for him there was no other option, and so I remained silent.

I asked Lupe about the boys and she told me that an uncle with papers had offered to take them across the border so they could see their father. It would be good for them to see him someplace besides the jail, she said, it would be good for them to be able to hug him. She added that she wished she could take the boys herself, that she wished she could see her husband with her own eyes.

A week later I checked in again with Lupe. Did the boys see José? I asked. Yes, she said, but not Vicente. He just got his arm put in a cast. He's a little sad, she explained, he hasn't seen his daddy since he was in court. Lupe told me that José was still at the border, that he planned to cross again soon, maybe this weekend, that everything was fine, that he told her not to worry.

Several days later Lupe sent a text message: José told me he'd cross Sunday to walk thru the desert but I'm worried now because it's been 3 days and I still haven't heard anything from him.

Then, a few days later: Buenos dias, José is back at the border, la migra chased him but his group scattered and they couldn't catch him, gracias a Dios. His body aches and he has a fever. He needs rest.

I DREAM THAT I AM AT WORK, THAT DIANE IS SITTING AT the bar drinking a latte. Look, Diane says, pointing through the open doors across the courtyard. It's José. I look out and see a gaunt man with a gray beard wandering slowly and aimlessly along the walkway. I leave the counter and make my way to him. He is wearing a black baseball hat and a gray shirt hangs loosely from his thin shoulders. José, I say. You're back. His eyes are sunken in their sockets, his face is dark and old. I've been in the desert, he says. There are things I could tell you.

I RAN INTO DIANE AND HER CHILDREN IN THE CHECKOUT line of the grocery store. Listen, she told me as she wrested a candy bar from the clutches of her five-year-old daughter, we want to give something to José's family for Christmas. The kids raised money at a bake sale and they want Lupe and the boys to have it. That's so sweet, I said. I looked down at Diane's daughter, twirling in circles beside the magazine rack. Do you have any idea what the boys like? Diane asked. I know they like soccer, I told her. I could get them a gift certificate to the soccer shop, she suggested. And maybe a certificate to Target for Lupe. She could get whatever she needs there, you know, things for the house, school supplies, clothes for the boys. I smiled. That'd be great, I said, I'm sure they'll really appreciate it. Diane reached out to stop her infant son, seated in the shopping cart, from ingesting a tube of lip balm. She sighed. Sorry, she said. If I give you the certificates later this week, do you think you could deliver them to Lupe for me? I don't speak any Spanish, she said, we won't be able to understand each other. I nodded. Of course, I said.

AT THE DOORSTEP OF HER TRAILER, LUPE SHIED AWAY FROM me as I held out the envelope to her. It's too much, she said, I can't take it. Diane's kids raised the money, I told her. They want you to have it. She breathed in and lifted her face toward the sky with a look of resignation. It's a gift, I told her, it's almost Christmas. Lupe squinted at the sun and then took the envelope and stared down at the ground. I don't know how to thank them, she said. Will you tell them how much I appreciate it?

Before I left, I asked Lupe about José. Oh, she said. Things are hard right now, un poco difícil. She told me José had crossed again a week ago and was caught by the Border Patrol. He didn't go to court, she said, they didn't send him to prison, but they bused him away, far from here, they deported him through Mexicali. I shook my head. They do that sometimes, I told her, to make it harder for them to cross in the same place again. Well, she said, he's still trying to get across, but there's some problems with the coyotes. What's the problem? I asked. Lupe interlaced her fingers in front of her stomach. It's just that he's afraid of them, tiene un poco miedo. She paused. I'm afraid too, she added.

I asked her what happened and she looked into the distance and began wringing her hands. What happened is that three or four days after José crossed, I still hadn't heard anything from him. One morning I got a call from this man who said they needed extra money to get José to the city. He said that José was in a safe house but that they needed a thousand dollars to bring him the rest of the way. I asked him to put José on the phone so I would know he was telling the truth, but the man said he wasn't with him. He told me that José was fine, that I should trust him, that they just needed an extra thousand dollars to finish the trip. I told the man to call me back when he could put José on the phone. I'll give the money once I talk to him, I said, and I hung up.

Lupe began to talk more slowly, drawing out her sentences, speaking through one side of her mouth. The rest of the morning I didn't know what to do with myself. I took the boys to school, I didn't tell them about the phone call. I came back home and for a while I just sat around the house trying to think of what to do. Finally I went out to take cash from the bank. I was shaking the whole time.

Later that same day, she continued, two men came to my door just before sundown. They told me that if I wanted José to make it home, I'd better give them the money right there. The boys were home from school by then, she said, they didn't know what to think. What was I supposed to do? She turned her palms up in a small gesture of surrender. I was scared, she said. She drew her shoulders around her neck and shook her head to one side and shuddered. I wanted to reach out and touch her.

The men took the money and left, Lupe continued. They said not to worry, that they'd bring José in the morning. I couldn't even sleep that night, I didn't know what to do. Lupe began wringing her hands again. By the next afternoon, they still hadn't come, so I dialed the same number they had called me from the day before. A different man answered this time. He told me he didn't know what I was talking about and he said I'd better calm down, that I'd better wait patiently, that if I knew what was good for me I wouldn't call again, and then he hung up. I felt so desperate, I was outside of myself.

Finally, late in the night, José called. He was in Mexicali, he had just been deported. He didn't know what I was talking about—he was never in a safe house, he was never with those men. He was so angry that he called the man who had made all the arrangements to smuggle him. What are you going to do with the money you took from my wife? he asked. Are you going to use it to get me back across the border, to bring me back to my family? The man claimed he didn't know what he was talking about, he told José he should think twice before making accusations, and then he warned him that he'd better not see him again, that if he saw him again he'd kill him.

Lupe was silent for a long time before finally shrugging her shoulders. José thinks it was just a threat, she said, just talk. He's back at the border now, but he's staying somewhere else, in a different part of town. She looked up again, squinting at the sun. He says he's safe there, but he doesn't go out much, he doesn't want to be seen in the streets, just to be sure.

I asked Lupe if José was planning to cross again. Yo creo que sí, she said. But the nights are cold right now, and he needs someone new to take him across. She rubbed her arms. He's going to wait awhile, I think, until the time is right, until he finds someone he can trust. I looked away and shook my head. I wanted to confess to her that I wished I had the courage to smuggle José myself, to ferry him safely through the desert, past the sensors and watchtowers, past the agents patrolling distant trails and dirt roads, past the highway checkpoints. I wished that I could drive with him seated next to me, listening to him tell of his love for his dead mother, for the green hills of Oaxaca, for the streets and archways of his village. I wished that we could drive together through the night, past faraway fields and prisons to the edge of the city, its lights shimmering and stretched out across the vast basin before us, that we could make our way through empty streets and abandoned intersections, past the courthouse and the mercado until we finally arrived at the barrio, at the trailer park, at the door of José's home where Lupe would lie sleeping with their three children, no longer afraid to wake.

ON CHRISTMAS EVE, I DROVE TO MY CHILDHOOD HOME TO BE with my mother. At night, we sat together around a small tree and each opened a single present. Afterward, we stayed in the living room drinking eggnog and brandy, drifting in and out of conversation. As the night wore on, my mother asked me about José. You still seem distant, she said. I stared at the glass bulbs hanging from the

plastic limbs of our artificial tree. I don't know what to do, I confessed. I feel pain, I feel hurt, but it isn't mine. My mother sat on the
couch across from me. It's like—I paused, looking around the room,
thinking of what to say. It's like I never quit, I finally muttered. It's
like I'm still a part of this thing that crushes. My mother made a
sound, like she was taking in a breath, like she was about to say
something. It's been almost four years since I left, I told her, but
when I'm in the courtroom, when I'm talking with the lawyers,
when I'm at the jail, it's like something inside of me still belongs to
it. I leaned forward and ran my hands through my hair.

You know, my mother said, it's okay to feel pain. Of course José's
pain isn't yours, of course his family's hurt isn't your hurt. But he's
your friend, so give yourself permission to grieve for him, permission to mourn that he cannot be here. I shook my head. But José's
situation is not unique. There are thousands of people just like him,
thousands of cases, thousands of families. Millions, actually—the
whole idea of it is suffocating. My mother nodded. It's true, she said,
but it's also true that for his family, and for you, José *is* unique. Sure
there might be thousands or millions of people in his position, but
it's because of him that their situation is no longer abstract to you.
You are no longer severed from what it means to send someone back
across the border. You know what's keeping him away, what keeps
him from his family. It's something close to you, something that's
become a part of you.

My mother took a long drink from her eggnog. You know, she
told me, the first job I ever had was at the Desert Museum in Tucson.

I was barely a teenager and all I wanted, more than anything else in the world, was to be around the animals. There was one man there, the curator of reptiles, who took me under his wing. He let me follow him through all the exhibits and let me help with feeding the animals and cleaning their cages. I remember watching him feed the snakes each day—he would take these little ground squirrels, grab them by the hind legs, and rap their heads against a countertop to quickly snap their necks. Then he would throw them right to the snakes, their bodies still warm and twitching. One day I tried to rescue one of the ground squirrels—I snuck it into my bag and brought it home. I tried taking care of it for days, until I eventually realized that I had failed, that the animal was dying, and that I was the one responsible for killing it. When the little squirrel could barely move, I finally took it up by its hind legs and tried to end its life the way I had seen the curator do it. I smashed it against a table and threw it onto the ground. When I finally got the courage to look down at its body, I realized that the little squirrel was still alive, that one of its eyes had popped out. I panicked and I grabbed it by the legs and slammed its head over and over again against the ground, crying until I knew it was finally dead.

My mother sighed and looked at my face. As I looked back at her, I realized that I had been clenching my teeth. I still carry that around with me, my mother said, I'll never forget it as long as I live. She looked down into her glass of eggnog. What I'm saying is that we learn violence by watching others, by seeing it enshrined in institutions. Then, even without choosing it, it becomes normal to us, it even becomes part of who we are. As my mother spoke she leaned forward, and I wondered if she would reach out to touch me.

The part of you that is capable of violence, she said, maybe you wish to be rid of it, to wash yourself of it, but it's not that easy. I sat back in my seat and stared up at the ceiling, listening to my mother's voice. You spent nearly four years on the border, she said. You weren't just observing a reality, you were participating in it. You can't exist within a system for that long without being implicated, without absorbing its poison. And let me tell you, it isn't something that's just going to slowly go away. It's part of who you've become. So what will you do? All you can do is try to find a place to hold it, a way to not lose some purpose for it all.

For a long while I looked down at my hands, trying to control the heat rising in my face. I thought about my dreams, about all the terrors I had never shared with her. Finally, I looked up at my mother and met her gaze. I had a dream José was back, I told her. He came in to work. He was skinny, his beard had grown out, his face was tired and worn. He had been in the desert for days, maybe a week or more, and he still seemed lost. It was like he had something to tell me, but I don't know what it was. My mother thought for a moment, leaning back on the couch. You know, she said, many cultures believe that our souls travel at night, that they leave the body to visit the people who care about them. So maybe José came to visit you. My mother took one last drink from her eggnog. Or maybe you need to visit him, she suggested, looking at me from across the room. Maybe you need to go to him and listen.

Mira, aquí la ley viene de los narcos. In the streets you can see them out on patrol. I've seen them myself, driving through the neighborhood in convoys, standing in the backs of trucks with guns and masks. Everyone who lives here knows who the bosses are, they know the local leaders by sight. If you talk in the street, if you say something against the narcos, people will hear you. Anyone could report you, you never know who's working for them. If someone is killed or kidnapped on the streets, no one sees anything. No one reports against them. Everyone here knows one another, everybody knows someone in the business, you see?

When someone new walks through the streets, the narcos know right away, they immediately find out who they are. They're always worried that other mafias are coming. For example, when you called me and said you wanted to visit, I went to Ignacio at the pawnshop down the street. I told him that a friend from my old job was coming to check in on me, to see how I'm doing. I told him casually, like it was nothing. But the real reason I told him is because he knows people, so when someone asks, Who was walking with José in the street this morning? Who went to talk with José at his house? he can tell them, Oh, don't worry, it was nobody, it was just José's friend from work.

I see all this and I think of my boys. For a while, you know, a couple months ago, after I had tried to cross again and again, I finally started to think that maybe my family could come live in Mexico until Lupe and I could arrange our papers. I even mentioned it to the boys on the phone. We don't want to live in Mexico, they told me. We don't know anyone there. We like it here, they said, we like our school. They bragged about how good they were doing in their classes. José Junior was on the phone telling me about his last report card. Dad, he said, I got pure A's with just one B. I did it to make you proud.

When I really started to think about it, I realized that, as a good father, I could never bring my boys here. I think a lot about the environment here in Mexico. Here it is normal for children to hear of murder. There's a school just down the street from here, I walk by it every day. I see the children in the schoolyard play at killing. Te voy a matar, they say to one another, soy pistolero, soy narco. So I think about the mentality my boys would be exposed to. I don't want my sons to grow up like this.

Things here can go very quickly from bad to worse. A kid's mentality can change very fast. They see that delinquency is easy, that they don't have to study to get money, to have success, and so they engage in drug work, they align themselves with the narcos even from a very young age.

Mexico could be a great country, a rich country, a country of opportunity. There are leaders in this country, but they are not given an education, they are not valued, they are ending up in the mafia. So you see, this sets up a cycle: How can a government care for its people if it is run by the mafia? And how can the mafia manage society if their leaders don't even have education? You know those forty-three students who went missing? They were studying at a rural college to become teachers. They disappeared more than a year ago and still no one knows what happened to them. Probably they were killed by narcos, by the cartel. They were accused of causing trouble because they were politically active, because they were protesting for better transportation, for more support from the local and state government. But the government is in the hands of the cartel, so it's not concerned with them, it doesn't protect them.

Those students would have grown to become teachers, they could have even been future doctors, future presidents. But in Mexico education means nothing. If our government valued those students, they would have made an investigation, they would have found the problem, they would take action to fix it, to make sure it never happens again. A government has to care for its citizens. People in government must strive to protect their fellow man. But we don't have a real government here. I won't bring my boys to live in this country.

In the U.S., at least the system is more organized, laws are respected, there is not so much corruption. The system there doesn't leave people uneducated, it doesn't leave them to die in hunger, to die without a name, without an investigation into their death. That's why I have always taught my boys to respect authority and to give thanks to the law, even to the police. For years I worked at a Chipotle. I started as the lowest worker, standing at the cash register, cleaning off the tables, sweeping up the floors. The police came in all the time to order food and I was always friendly with them. They started to recognize me—after a while they even learned my name. Eventually I worked my way up in the restaurant to become the main cook. Everyone I worked with said I was the best cook they'd ever seen, that I could do the work of two men. The policemen would see me cooking in the back and yell to me. What's up, José, how's it going? One time I came into the restaurant on my day off to pick up my paycheck. I was with my boys and when we walked in, there was a table full of police officers having lunch. They stood up to shake my hand. José, they said, it's good to see you, are these your boys? They even shook my boys' hands. My boys, they couldn't believe it. After we left, Diego said to me, how do those cops know you, dad? We're friendly to one another, I told him, that's all. We treat each other with respect.

The other day I was on the phone with Diego, he was telling me that he wanted to change classes, complaining that he thought his teacher was racist against him because he's Mexican. I told him, you must learn to do what your teacher says. If you think she is racist, talk with your family, meet with your teacher. You cannot give up just because you think someone is against you, because it is difficult to face them. I try to teach my boys that they must not be consumed by battle, they must not give in to vice, they must work hard to become someone in life.

When Lupe and I went to get married, the pastor told us that it was important to grow a family, that it was important for children to see their parents together. Es de mucho valor una familia unida. Family should stay together. If I must stay in Mexico and my wife raises my boys alone, they will be getting less care, less love, and so the family will slowly deteriorate. Being a parent is a job that you share, it's a job you have to be present for. When I was in jail, the same place where you brought the boys to see me, I was with many others that had returned to Mexico to be with their dying family members, people with family in the United States, family on both sides. I began to see that when people are separated from their families, many of them fall into depression or fall to other illnesses. One man in the prison, a man in my same situation, told me that his wife became so depressed while he was away that she collapsed and had to be taken to the hospital.

Some politicians in the United States think that if a mother or father is deported, this will cause the entire family to move back to Mexico. But in fact, the mothers and fathers with the best family values will want their family to stay in the U.S., they will cross the border again and again to be with them. So you see, these same people, the ones with the most dedication to their family, they begin to build up a record of deportation, they have more and more problems with the government, and it becomes harder and harder for them to ever become legal. In this way, the U.S. is making criminals out of those who could become its very best citizens.

I owe a lot to the U.S., you know, I really do. The United States has given me a lot. My mother built her house in Oaxaca with the money I earned from working there. I feel that I have been blessed there, so I don't want to have problems with the government. I want to legalize, I want to get a lawyer. I want to become a citizen.

To be honest, I am still grateful to the United States. If I am arrested crossing the border, I understand it's part of the system. I realize that I am crossing illegally. But it's complicated, you see. I know I'm breaking the rules, but it is necessary because my family is there. I don't want to cause harm to the country, but I have to break the law. I have to. Es una necesidad. It is a situation of emotion, of love. Those who accept staying apart from their family are without love. Their children grow up without love. So I must fight against this.

I know there are laws, I know that they need to be enforced, but at the same moment these laws are wounding me, wounding something inside me. My children want me there, my wife wants me there, all of them are pleading for me to stay, but the government is separating us. If I search my feelings, I don't feel hate but sadness. The day you saw me in court, the day I saw my family there, it was as if the government was destroying my family, tearing it apart right in front of me. I could feel the power they held over us.

I shouldn't have left the U.S., it's true. I shouldn't have left my family, but I couldn't live without going to see my mother. I remember thinking to myself, if my mother is dying and I have the ability to be by her side, I must do it. It was not a choice for me, there was no other way. And that's why I'm here, because I had too much love for my mother. Now I sit in this room and I look out the window at those hills. Those hills that you see right there, that's the United

States. I used to be able to just run up and over those hills. But now there is a barrier. I hate it, I hate it. It's something barbaric.

The crossing now, it's much more dangerous than it ever was. It's not easy. I've tried four times in six months and still I can't get across. Each time it takes something from you. And of course, each time it takes money. People in my situation, people who have tried again and again to get across, they become desperate. They try to find an easier way to get across, a cheaper way. Out of desperation, I've even thought of crossing over as a mule for the cartels. It's cheaper that way, you know. The coyotes give you a bundle of marijuana to carry on your back and you pay them half of what you would pay anywhere else. You cross with a group of mules and your coyote is guided the whole time by the scouts watching from the hilltops, so there's less chance you get caught. If you arrive successfully at the other side, they give you a payment. You get back the money you paid them and sometimes you even make money. But it's a risk, of course. If you are captured by la migra you are entered in the computer as a drug trafficker, and you'll never be able to become legal. The cartel will be against you too, because you lost their load. You become a victim of both systems.

I don't want to carry drugs across the desert, I don't want to get myself into more problems, but sometimes it's not a choice. The same people who control the drug smuggling control the human trafficking, so in some places if you want to get across, you have to carry a load. I've even heard that sometimes they will kill you if you refuse. A man in jail told me that there are mass graves in the desert where many people are buried for this very reason.

I met another man in jail, a man from Michoacán who crossed with a group of eighty-five. Each time the group stopped, he would count their numbers, and each time the number was less. There was a woman in the group who was crossing with her five-year-old daughter. The girl was exhausted, she wanted water and there was none. The man from Michoacán offered to carry the girl on his shoulders and the woman thanked him. After a while, he noticed that the girl had not moved or said anything so he took her off his shoulders and saw that she was dead. The mother, of course, she was beside herself, she became hysterical. The coyotes told them that the group had to keep going, that they must leave the girl's body there. The man argued with them. I'll carry her body myself, he said. Two or three miles later, the girl's mother died too. The man fought with the coyotes. We have to bury them, he said, we have to tell someone they're here. No, they said, we have to keep going. Come with us or stay behind, you decide. The man shouted and wept. You're criminals, he told the coyotes, you are evil. He did everything he could to remember where they left the bodies, to guard the image of that place in his mind.

Later, when the group arrived at the road, they were picked up in trucks and vans. The man from Michoacán ended up in a truck that got chased down the highway by police. Two migrants fell from the back of the truck during the chase, he said, and he never knew of them again. The driver evaded the police and delivered the migrants to a drop house where they were held for ransom. Some of them were taken into another room and tortured or killed. After several days some men began to fight with the smugglers and one of them broke a window and escaped. The police found him and he told them about the drop house, and soon the place was raided by immigration agents, the smugglers were arrested, the migrants were processed for deportation. The man from Michoacán told the agents about the girl and her mother, he told them he knew where to find them. The agents took the man in a helicopter through the desert and then, believe it or not, he found the place. On the ground they found the body of the woman already decomposing. The animals had been at the body. The little girl was there too, but she was missing a leg. He told me that even the agents began to cry. The man from Michoacán was peaceful, he was a family man like me. But he told me that if he ever found one of those men, if he ever saw one of those coyotes, he would kill them.

So you see, each time I cross I risk my life. When you step into the Mexican consulate, you see pictures of the missing. All of us who cross are exposed to this possibility. We know there are dangers in the desert and in the mountains. La mafia, la migra. There's mountain lions, snakes. There's cliffs and deep canyons. There's no water. There are many dangers, but for me it doesn't matter. I have to cross, I have to arrive to the other side. I even dream that I am there. I dream that I'm there with my family, that it's morning and I have to go to work. Then I wake up and I'm here.

The judges in the United States, if they know the reality, they know they are sending people to their death. They are sending people to commit suicide. I will do anything to be on the other side. To be honest, I would rather be in prison in the U.S. and see my boys once a week through the glass than to stay here and be separated from my family. At least I would be closer to them. So you see, there is nothing that can keep me from crossing. My boys are not dogs to be abandoned in the street. I will walk through the desert for five days, eight days, ten days, whatever it takes to be with them. I'll eat grass, I'll eat bushes, I'll eat cactus, I'll drink filthy cattle water, I'll drink nothing at all. I'll run and hide from la migra, I'll pay the mafias whatever I have to. They can take my money, they can rob my family, they can lock me away, but I will keep coming back. I will keep crossing, again and again, until I make it, until I am together again with my family. No, no me quedo aquí. Voy a seguir intentando pasar.

EPILOGUE

On a hot Texas evening at the edge of Big Bend National Park, I watched a man ride his horse across the Rio Grande. After traversing a riverbank teeming with locusts, he ushered his horse up the small hill where I stood overlooking the darkening valley. Buenas tardes, I greeted him. He eyed me from his saddle. You speak good Spanish, he said, are you la migra? No, I answered. A ranger? No, I assured him, just a tourist.

I gestured at the village across the river and asked the man if he lived in Boquillas. Of course, he said, beaming with pride. I asked what he did for work and he nodded at the unattended souvenirs and handmade crafts that had been set out atop the rocks. No hay trabajo, he complained—we make our money from tourists.

I asked if many Americans crossed over to visit. Sure, he said, Boquillas is very safe. Narcos don't bother us, even the rangers and la migra leave us alone. He paused. You know, he said, there's a nice restaurant in my village. Is there breakfast? I asked. Of course, he smiled. I'll come for you in the morning.

As the man rode back across the valley, the rugged Sierra del Carmen, formed by the shifting of ancient seas and the endless faulting of the earth's crust, smoldered pink with the last light of the day.

The next morning, as the sun grew pale and white in the eastern sky, I met my guide at the banks of the river. He instructed me to climb onto his horse, and then, like it was nothing, he spurred the animal across the river into Mexico. We spoke little as I jostled atop sauntering haunches and grasped at the back of his saddle. Passing the first cinderblock homes of Boquillas, I considered the extent to which my safekeeping depended upon this stranger, leading me into the silent and unfamiliar streets of his village.

I ate breakfast alone on a shaded patio, where I observed the passing of rumbling trucks and tired-looking horses as Boquillas slowly woke to the day. After breakfast, as we rode back toward the border, I asked my guide about violence in the surrounding towns and villages. He shook his head. The delincuentes don't come to Boquillas. If they mess with someone here they won't even make it to the edge of the village. He looked back at me over his shoulder. Here the law comes from the people. We look out for one another, me entiendes?

As the horse approached the border I questioned my guide about the crossing. Aren't there cameras? I asked. Sensors? No, he said. Está tranquilo. As we came closer, I scanned the ridge above the riverbank, half expecting to hear the roar of a vehicle or the shouts of silhouetted men—but there was only the slow snaking of the river, the faint sound of water drifting by on its journey through deep canyons and broad basins, past irrigated fields and sprawling floodplains, toward the vast and shimmering waters of the Gulf.

Later that morning I set out to visit Boquillas Canyon. At the trailhead, I read several safety notices. Pack sufficient drinking water. Beware of snakes. Do not purchase souvenirs from border merchants. Do not cross the Rio Grande. Always let someone know where you're going and when you expect to return.

The trail into Boquillas Canyon ended at the terminus of a riverbank where the water met a vertical limestone wall. I removed my shirt and lowered myself into the gentle current of the Rio Grande, my muscles tensing at its coolness. Above me the canyon walls hummed like a generator and two falcons circled in sun-heated air. I reached my arms deep into the wet sediment that had settled at the bottom of the riverbed. The waters of the river flowed pale and brown, liquid earth washing over me like so many human hands, like a skin unending.

As I swam toward a bend in the canyon, the river became increasingly shallow. In a patch of sunlight, two longnose gars, relics of the Paleozoic era, hovered in the silted waters. I stood to walk along the adjacent shorelines, crossing the river time and again as each bank came to an end, until finally, for one brief moment, I forgot in which country I stood. All around me the landscape trembled and breathed as one.

AUTHOR'S NOTE

During the years I was at work on *The Line Becomes a River*, I always imagined it would come to exist as a document of an uglier time, a past recognizably worse than the present. This thought was rooted in the seductive idea that ours is a society moving always in the direction of justice, one that gradually lurches forward toward greater civil and human rights. This I now recognize as wishful thinking, rooted in the same naivety that underlay my decision to join the Border Patrol more than a decade ago. This is the naivety that so often grips people who are young and idealistic, causing us to overestimate ourselves and underestimate institutions of power, allowing us to believe that we might work to change them from within, that by witnessing the violence they perpetrate, we might learn to subvert it without participating in it ourselves.

Today, instead of looking back on an uglier time, we see a border that has become ever more militarized, ever more deadly for migrants, ever more dismissive of their lives and indifferent to their suffering. The U.S.-Mexico border, I have learned, is a place that perpetually shatters naivety, a place where idealism withers in the face of a violent status quo that is constantly being normalized, minimized, or ignored. But even as an adult stripped, in large part, of my youthful illusions, to watch this cherished place descend into its current grim reality, all while knowing that I participated in the transformation, has been like watching a loved one slip into the grip of an incurable disease for which I myself served as a carrier.

This current state of crisis did not descend from nowhere. For as long as many of us can remember, the border has been depicted as a place out of control, overrun by criminality. In the narrative that has dominated the national consciousness, violence and disorder are endemic to the region and those who are drawn to it. When words like *border* or *migrant* are uttered, they carry this narrative with them, along with a sense of obscure menace to people and places far from the country's frontier: loss of jobs, encroaching violence, the erosion of a familiar dominant culture. What we have long been made to look away from, however, are the places most affected by a militarized border, and the migrants who are most impacted by the narrative that has so long excluded their experience.

In the summer of 2018, as major media outlets began to cover stories of family separation following the implementation of the Trump administration's "zero tolerance" immigration policy, Americans were finally made to grapple with the human cost of border enforcement at a national level. Perhaps unsurprisingly, the greatest public outcry came in response to viral photographs that distilled the policy's cruelty into sharable images of children crying out at the feet of armed border guards and sleeping on bare floors behind cages. For once the public responded to the news with swift and widespread condemnation that crossed partisan lines, forcing the president to issue an executive order reversing the practice of family separation.

Because we are rightly habituated to believe in the innocence of children, because the "othering" of a child requires a special degree of callousness, these images and stories proved difficult to shake off—they caused us to feel, for one reverberating moment, a sense of horror at beholding our nation, our institutions, and perhaps even ourselves. But the separation of families does not represent one isolated, horrifying event in our history; it is merely a chilling extension of the dehumanizing policies that came before it.

One of my principal goals in *The Line Becomes a River* was to create space for readers to inhabit an emergent sense of horror at the suffering that takes place every day at the border. In narrating my own gradual participation in the various degrees of violence inflicted in the fulfillment of our nation's immigration policies and enforcement practices, I sought to leave room for readers to construct their own moral interpretation of the events described. While the book does offer contextual pieces of history and research, it does not attempt to make sense of the current political moment, nor does it endeavor to explain the politics that led to it—it seeks to function as literature rather than reportage, to resonate more deeply within the soul than in the mind.

When I left the Border Patrol in 2012, it had not yet occurred to me to write publicly about my experiences there. As I settled into a new life, however, I began revisiting the journals I had kept during my years on the job as a way to make sense of where I had been, what I had seen, what I had done and not done. When I began, in the ensuing years, to conceive of a book, I knew that it would need to be anchored in an exploration of the many manifestations of border violence. This became, in part one, a depiction of the violence wrought by the policing of desert crossings; in part two, an examination of the commodification of migrants' lives and the drug war violence that so often spurs their flight from home; and in part three, an intimate portrait of the threat that hovers ceaselessly over migrants, even long after they establish lives in a new country—a threat always poised to come knocking at the door.

Writing was also a way of charting my own involvement with an institution largely indifferent to human life, an opportunity to finally grapple with all the ways I had normalized the layered violence that is inseparable from border enforcement. Freed from the everyday need to dissociate my duties from my sense of compassion and humanity, I was able to trace my own doubts and unease about the work I had done, the same way one might identify in retrospect the initially unnoticed symptoms of a psychological disorder.

Traveling through the borderlands in the years after I left the Border Patrol, I became reacquainted with the region as a civilian and saw with fresh eyes how the work in which I had been involved weighed heavy on the landscape. Living near the border means becoming conditioned to a degree of militarization and surveillance that would cause great alarm in any other part of the country. At immigration checkpoints between distant desert towns, automated cameras snap mugshots of you behind the wheel, and uniformed agents nod at drivers with light skin, waving them on to "Have a nice day," while requiring those who are darker to prove their status, to explain their presence, and often, to step out of their vehicles while agents rummage through their belongings and invite drug-sniffing dogs to crawl across their car seats. On the open highway, you pass multitudes of green-striped patrol vehicles driving in either direction, often too many to keep count. Signs warn of "Danger" and advise "Travel Not Recommended," cautioning travelers that "Smuggling and Illegal Immigration May Be Encountered In This Area" or "Visitors May Encounter Armed Criminals and Smuggling Vehicles Traveling at High Rates of Speed." Observation towers and trucks equipped with radar and infrared cameras can be seen stationed upon surrounding hilltops, monitoring the desert in every direction. Away from roads, if you are bold enough to go hiking on desert trails, you might encounter low-flying helicopters overhead, reporting your location to nearby agents.

In the borderlands you become conditioned, above all, to living with an ever-present sense of unease, of being watched, of moving through a landscape that has been resignified as a transitional terrain—a place made to exist, literally and figuratively, at the margins. To inhabit such a place is to inhabit a state of in-between-ness, a space where the ground is aggressively claimed, but the people who belong to it, and those seeking to cross it, are rejected. This is a place that Chicana scholar and theorist Gloria Anzaldúa describes as "an unstable, unpredictable, precarious, always-in-transition space lacking clear boundaries," a place she refers to using the Nahuatl word for middle space, *nepantla*. "Living in this liminal zone," she writes, "means being in a constant state of displacement."

It is important to remember, however, that the borderlands were not always liminal, that this state of displacement was imposed by a political boundary that resulted from war. The modern-day torments that grip this place must be understood as part of this history, rooted in conquest and the thirst for empire. In his book *Columbus and Other Cannibals,* Native American scholar Jack D. Forbes suggests that the violent historical trajectory of colonial and postcolonial America should be understood as stemming from a kind of sickness—what he calls "the *wétiko* disease." In the language of the Cree people, *wétikos* are individuals or spirits who terrorize others through evil acts. Forbes posits that Columbus, the conquistadors, and the waves of colonizers who followed them were all *wétikos,* carriers of a cannibalistic psychosis he defines as "the disease of aggression against other living things . . . the disease of the consuming of other creatures' lives and possessions."

Forbes explains that over the centuries since it was first introduced, this highly contagious disease of exploitation has gradually become more subtle, but no less pervasive. It often manifests, he suggests, simply as a dull sense of fear, leading to participation in acts of terror that have been so normalized by the dominant culture as to be scarcely recognizable as such at all. "We are made to be crazy," Forbes writes, "by other people who are also crazy and who draw for us a map of the world which is ugly, negative, fearful." The *wétiko* disease is, above all, an affliction of the psyche and spirit that causes us to become "passive foot-soldiers trained to surrender [our] minds and hearts." On a societal level, it manifests both in the relentless move toward militarization and in our blind acceptance of this path as inevitable and necessary.

Forbes also writes of the long-standing *wétiko* urge to "desanctify" places that have historically been regarded as holy, sacred, and beautiful by native people. He writes, "The significance of desanctifying the earth, the animals, the plants, the trees, and even human beings is that the world is made a potentially ugly and very exploitable place." This describes, in part, the mentality that has allowed the two-thousand-mile-long border region to be transformed into a vast "buffer zone," a geography that has itself been converted into a tool of enforcement that is considered so disposable as to merit being riven by an immense wall—seven hundred miles of which already exists.

In the mid-2000s, the Italian philosopher Giorgio Agamben traced the history of the concept known as the "state of exception." In the name of "security," governments have for centuries used this political tool of power to suspend or diminish the rights and protections of certain people, in certain places, usually in response to perceived emergencies or crises. Agamben was particularly interested in our post-9/11 era, in which the suspension of traditional rights and protections has been prolonged indefinitely for individuals such as "enemy combatants" in the War on Terror, who are detained in ways that deviate entirely from the supposed inalienable rights established by the Geneva Conventions and U.S. legal norms. Agamben describes these people as being at once bound by, and abandoned to, law.

In Agamben's framework, the U.S.-Mexico border can be understood as a vast zone of exception, a place where laws and rights are applied differently than in any other part of the nation. Since 9/11, presidents of both parties have deployed National Guard troops there in response to ill-defined crises. When troops were deployed to the border by President Trump, for example, in April 2018, crossings were at historic lows, and the U.S. border was, by almost any measure, more secure than at any point in recent decades—though we might ask, secure for whom?

The borderlands have slowly become a place where citizens are subject to distinct standards for search and detention, and where due process for noncitizens is often unrecognizable as anything that might exist within the American legal system. It is a place where migrants are regularly sentenced through mass hearings in which the fates of as many as seventy-five individuals can be adjudicated one after another in a matter of minutes, after which they are funneled into a burgeoning immigration incarceration complex. It is a landscape often written off as a "wasteland" that is inherently "hostile"—without recognition that it has, in fact, been *made* to be hostile. Violence does not grow organically in our deserts or at our borders. It has arrived there through policy.

The deadly transformation of our southwestern borderlands began in the 1990s, when Border Patrol chiefs began cracking down on migrant crossings in heavily trafficked urban areas like El Paso and San Diego. Walls were built, budgets ballooned, and scores of new agents were hired to patrol border towns. Everywhere else, it was assumed, the inhospitable desert would do the dirty work of deterring crossers away from the public eye.

Doris Meissner, the commissioner of the Immigration and Naturalization Service from 1993 to 2000, told *The Arizona Republic* that during the adoption of this strategy, which came to be known as "Prevention Through Deterrence," enforcement officials and policy makers believed "that geography would be an ally to us" and that border crossings "would go down to a trickle once people realized what it's like." But migrants continued to cross despite the new dangers of the journey, endangering their lives in the desert in ways they had never done before. Even as it became obvious that large numbers of people were risking the crossing, resulting in an unprecedented number of deaths in increasingly remote corners of the desert, the government did not change course. "I will be absolutely frank with you," Meissner told an interviewer when asked to look back on the policy of deterrence in light of migrant deaths—"The idea of abandoning any kind of strengthened border enforcement because of that consequence was not a point of serious discussion."

Meissner's damning admission—that the sustained loss of hundreds of migrant lives on America's doorstep each year was not enough to cause the government to re-evaluate policy—reveals the extent to which the desert has been weaponized against migrants, and lays bare the fact that the hundreds who continue to die there every year are losing their lives *by design*. Deterrence-based enforcement has steered the immigration politics of every administration since that of President Clinton, and has resulted in an official tally of more than six thousand migrant deaths along the southern border between 2000 and 2016. This figure, it should be said, does nothing to account for the thousands more who have been reported as disappeared and never found, not to mention those whose disappearances are never reported in the first place.

Jason De León, in his book *The Land of Open Graves*, argues that the government views undocumented migrants as people "whose lives have no political or social value" and "whose deaths are of little consequence." This devaluation of migrant life is not just rhetorical: in 2018, investigative reporter Bob Ortega revealed that negligent tallying practices by the Border Patrol had failed to account for more than five hundred migrant deaths reported by medical examiners, landowners, and local law enforcement agencies over the last sixteen years. Those five hundred lives were, quite literally, erased from official records. De León writes that, for the families of the missing and disappeared, the ambiguity of their loss "freezes the grief process and renders closure impossible." The lack of a body not only prevents the proper rites of mourning and burial from being observed in the deceased's home community, but also "allows the perpetrators of violence plausible deniability."

In defense of its enforcement practices, the Border Patrol often touts its search-and-rescue operations as evidence of the agency's humanitarian priorities. I myself once clung to this argument— indeed it was even part of my motivation for joining. As an agent, I signed up to receive EMT training and allowed myself to cling to the idea that I was helping migrants by administering aid, even as I suppressed doubts about the job and ignored the ways my work helped push migrants toward death. In this respect, for the Border Patrol to demand recognition for saving lives is much like firefighters asking to be thanked for putting out a blaze started by their own chief. To paint the Border Patrol as a rescue operation is also to gloss over a pervasive culture of callousness and destruction: while I indeed worked alongside some deeply compassionate and honorable agents, I also witnessed coworkers scatter migrant groups in remote areas and destroy their water supplies without ever being held to account. (These practices have been extensively documented by humanitarian groups and recorded in "The Disappeared Report" compiled by No More Deaths and La Coalición de Derechos Humanos.)

For the majority of Americans, most of what happens on the border continues to remain out of sight and out of mind. But politicized immigration rhetoric now reaches into every corner of the nation, casting migrants as "animals," "gang members," and "rapists" while linking border security to vague notions of warfare and defense against invasion. The institutional culture of the Border Patrol has long been a product of such rhetoric and militarized thinking. Agents refer to migrants as "criminals," "aliens," "illegals," "bodies" or "toncs" (a slur with dubious origins, either an acronym standing for "temporarily out of native country" or a reference to the sound of a Maglite hitting a migrant's skull). They are equipped with drones, helicopters, infrared cameras, radar, ground sensors, Humvees, and explosion-resistant vehicles. The agency's practices divert crossers through some of the most deadly and difficult-to-traverse terrain in North America in order to provide agents with every conceivable advantage over those seeking entry into the U.S., people they are made to understand as *criminals* in the same way soldiers are made to understand those positioned against them as *enemies.*

This logic, rooted in the dehumanizing rhetoric of war, has transformed the border into a permanent zone of exception where some of the most vulnerable people on earth face death and disappearance on a daily basis, where children have been torn from their parents to send the message *You are not safe here, you are not welcome.* In this sense, the true crisis at the border is not one of surging crossings or growing criminality, but of our own increasing disregard for human life. To describe what we are seeing as a "crisis," however, is to imply that our current moment is somehow more horrifying than those that set the stage for it—moments that, had we allowed ourselves to see them and be horrified by them, might have prevented our arrival here in the first place.

In examining the power of political rhetoric to dehumanize migrants, it is also necessary to consider the ways our discourse dismisses the places and situations they come from, diminishing the very realities of their lives. In her critique of America's quest for retribution in the Middle East following the attacks of 9/11, the philosopher Judith Butler describes the process of *derealization* and its discursive power to create "humans not recognized as humans." In explaining how "certain lives are not considered lives at all," she turns to the example of obituaries, the primary form through which lost lives are humanized and recognized in the Western world—"the means by which a life becomes noteworthy." Butler notes the glaring absence of any such remembrances for victims of U.S. attacks in Afghanistan and Iraq, the profound unavailability of images, frames, stories, or names. "If there were to be an obituary," Butler writes, "there would have had to have been a life, a life worth noting, a life worth valuing and preserving, a life that qualifies for recognition."

The same is true, of course, for migrants who die on U.S. soil, on the very doorstep of our nation, and it is similarly true for migrants all across the globe. In an essay examining the omnipresence of modern borders and the immigration crisis in the Mediterranean, British journalist Frances Stonor Saunders argues that documents such as passports and visas are central components to how our society values and recognizes human life. "Identity is established by identification," Saunders writes, "and identification is established by documenting and fixing the socially significant and codifiable information that confirms who you are." Those who possess such documentation possess a *verified self*, "an identity, formed through and confirmed by identification, that is attested to be 'true.'"

As residents of the "first world," we are unthinkingly privileged in our possession of a verified self—it means, if nothing else, that our names are known to history, that our deaths will be recorded. Possessing freedom of movement frees us from the burden of a migrant identity, frees us from the fear that our lives might become defined by undocumented-ness and pervaded by the constant threat of arrest, deportation, and anonymity. "A war on immigration," Saunders argues, can also be understood as "a war on the global wanderings of the unverified self."

In 2013, shortly after his election to the papacy, Pope Francis paid visit to Lampedusa, the small Italian island in the Mediterranean commonly recognized as North Africa's "gateway to Europe." The island, only seventy miles from the shores of Tunisia, is a central destination point on the world's deadliest migrant route, where more than twenty thousand migrants have lost their lives attempting to cross the Mediterranean Sea. During his visit, the pontiff commemorated these deaths with a homily in which he referred to deceased migrants not as undifferentiated, derealized "others," but as family. "These brothers and sisters of ours were trying to escape difficult situations to find some serenity and peace; they were looking for a better place for themselves and their families, but instead they found death."

Standing at an altar assembled from remnants of wooden refugee boats, Pope Francis looked out over the port of Lampedusa and asked his audience, "Has any one of us grieved for the death of these brothers and sisters? Has any one of us wept?" He went on to ask, "Who is responsible for this blood?"—observing that "today no one in our world feels responsible. . . . We have become used to the suffering of others. . . . The globalization of indifference makes us all 'unnamed,' responsible, yet nameless and faceless."

Francis Stonor Saunders calls attention to the Pope's words in order to highlight the parallel anonymities that have come to define immigration crises across the globe: the privileged are as diffuse and unaccountable as the downtrodden are indistinct and unnamable. The stories of migrants become "infinitely reproducible to the point of abstraction," she writes, while the verified masses of the first world "remain unseeing and unseeable behind the high wall we have built to protect ourselves from the disordered, unauthorized, unregistered others beyond."

To push back against the abstraction of migrants' stories, to reject the dismissal and erasure of their lives, we must begin by grieving their deaths, by speaking their names, by seeing them, hearing them, and amplifying their voices. The Mexican intellectual Sayak Valencia, who hails from the border city of Tijuana, writes that "in order to change the order of things, it's crucial to cease behaviors that ally us with the cult of violence." She continues, "It is crucial to speak of the body, of the violence enacted upon it and suffered within it. . . . We have to be able to construct meaning around the death of any person. To make sure that the death and the pain of an Other cause a shudder in all of our bodies."

If our understanding of violence and death along the border can become something visceral, then we may begin to feel, deep within ourselves, no matter how far we live from the border, that what happens there is profoundly unnatural. "'Naturalizing' the conditions of a particular territory," Valencia warns, "leads to mystification and leaves us in an acritical and resigned position, negating the possibility that our actions might re-shape that supposedly essential 'nature' of the place." By collapsing the distance that separates us from the border, we might push back against the idea of its inherent violence, against the unceasing negation of its culture and people, against its continual transformation into a hellscape designed to repel migrants.

In 1992, Jorge Durand, a social anthropologist and geographer at Mexico's University of Guadalajara, coordinated a series of in-depth interviews with Mexican migrants who had experienced the hard journey to the United States. One of these migrants, a man named Aurelio, crossed the US border dozens of times, only to be captured and sent home by U.S. authorities on every single occasion. "El Norte es como el mar," he told his interviewer. "The north is like the sea." He went on to explain, "When I hear people speak of the United States, I am quickly made to think of the ocean. . . . When one travels as an illegal, he is dragged like the tail of an animal, like trash. I imagined how the sea washes trash onto the shore, and I told myself, maybe here it's just like I'm in the ocean, being tossed out again and again."

What we must understand about Aurelio is that his sense of being regarded as trash is in direct relation to our indifference, to the privileges that have been constructed for us at the expense and exclusion of him and others like him. At the same time, we must recognize that to feel empathy for him and others like him is not enough. "Compassion," Susan Sontag famously declared, "is an unstable emotion. It needs to be translated into action, or it withers." The same can be said of empathy—we can imagine Aurelio's pain, we can feel something that perhaps approaches it, and we can even, as Pope Francis suggests, grieve for him, weep for him—but in the end our feelings and our tears are useless unless they compel us to act in a way that might someday improve his situation. The hard truth is that the policies and structures that have taken Aurelio's body and rejected it, time and again, will remain in place until we push firmly against them, demanding they be abandoned or remade.

Derrick Jensen, a philosopher and radical environmentalist influenced by Jack D. Forbes and his theory of the *wétiko* psychosis, writes that "the responsibility for holding destructive institutions— more broadly systems, and more broadly yet cultures—accountable falls on each of us . . . This means that all of us who care about life need to force accountability onto those who do not; we must learn to be accountable to ourselves, our consciences, our neighbors, and the nonhuman members of our community . . . rather than be loyal to political, economic, religious, penal, educational, and other institutions that do not serve us well." With regard to our borders and the crises of migrant death and disappearance across the globe, we must thus declare loyalty to human life over shifting and mutable laws and policies, and we must remain attuned to these loyalties so as not to return to indifference.

When the violent shortcomings of our institutions are revealed, when their dehumanizing design is laid bare, it can be overwhelming to imagine navigating the particulars of enacting change. But what I have learned from giving myself over to a structure of power, from living within its grim vision and helping to cannibalize the people and places from which I came, is that small impulses and interactions have the power to lead us back toward humanity, and heeding them can be a means of extricating ourselves from systems of thought and policy that perpetuate detachment. We can do this in spite of all the mechanisms that have been devised to keep us wedded to individual and nationalistic self-interest. As obvious as it might seem, to truly and completely reject a culture of violence, to banish it from our hearts and souls, we must first fully refuse to participate in it, and refuse to partake in its normalization. When we consider the border, we might think of our home; when we consider those who cross it, we might think of those we hold dear.

Tucson, Arizona

December 2018

ACKNOWLEDGMENTS

For their mentorship: Alison Deming, Luis Urrea, Adela Licona, Ander Monson, Fenton Johnson, Chris Cokinos, Manuel Muñoz, Susan Briante, Farid Matuk, Bob Houston, Gary Paul Nabhan, Terry Wimmer, Sandra Cisneros, Dr. Clarissa Pinkola-Estés, Phil Klay, Alfredo Corchado, Marcel Oomen, Linda Pietersen, Floris Vermeulen, and the entire University of Arizona Creative Writing faculty.

For their camaraderie: Page Buono, Joseph Bradbury, Jan Bindas-Tenny, Taneum Bambrick, Lauren Markham, Hernan Diaz, Javier Zamora, and all my colleagues among the Bread Loaf waiters of 2016, The Bread Loaf fellows of 2018, the University of Arizona MFA cohorts of 2014 through 2017.

For faithfully steering this book through the world: Rebecca Gradinger, Becky Saletan, Jynne Dilling, Glory Plata, Katie Freeman, Alan Walker, Jennifer Huang, May-Zhee Lim, Michelle Koufopoulos, Veronica Goldstein, Stuart Williams, Joe Pickering, and the staffs of Fletcher & Company, The Bodley Head, and Riverhead Books.

For their professional encouragement and careful direction: Michael Collier, Rick Bass, David Shields, Wendy Walters, Antonìo Ruiz-Camacho, John Vaillant, Brian Blanchfield, Valeria Luiselli, Beowulf Sheehan, Molly Molloy, Pedro Serrano, Katherine Silver, y mi tocayo Francisco Goldman.

For kindly guiding me through the publishing landscape: Matt Weiland, Geoff Shandler, Jim Rutman, Fiona McCrae, Steve Woodward, Stephen Morrison, Ben George, Ed Winstead, Ladette Randolph, Robert Atwan, Jonathan Franzen, Scott Gast, H. Emerson Blake, Jennifer Sahn, Josalyn Knapic, Megan Kimble, Adam Berlin, and Jeffrey Heiman.

For financial support and opportunity: the Whiting Foundation, the Katherine Bakeless Nason Endowment, the Fulbright Program, the Banff Centre, the Agnese Nelms Haury Program in Environment and Social

Justice, the University of Arizona Poetry Center, the University of Arizona Institute for the Environment, the University of Amsterdam Institute for Migration and Ethnic Studies, and the Migration Policy Institute.

For fostering my early curiosities about migration and borders: Amy Oliver, Marie Piñeiro, Jack Childs, Daniel Hernández, Todd Eisenstadt, Stephen Randall, Gordon Appleby, Robert Pastor, Margie McHugh, Demetrios Papademetriou, and Deborah Meyers.

For helping me reconnect with the landscape of my youth: Eric Brunnemann and Elizabeth Jackson at Guadalupe Mountains National Park.

For their urgent work as translators and poets: Jen Hofer and John Pluecker.

For his steady psychological guidance and wisdom: Dr. Stephen Joseph.

For their generosity and sense of place: Bill Broyles and Keith Marroquin.

For their friendship: Sarah Steinberg, Scott Buchanan, Daisy Pitkin, Michael Versteeg, Kyle Farley, Addison Matthew, Patrick Callaway, Spenser Jordan Palmer, Kris Karlsson, Dewey Nelson, Daniel Troup, Ryan Olinger, Harry Manny, Erik and Dan Schmahl, Holly Hall, Alyson Head, Ryne Warner, Tracy Rose Guajardo, Jacqueline Brackeen, Matthew Thomas, Matthew Chovanec, John Washington, Julian Etienne, Karina Hernández, Stephan Oliver, Yolanda Morales, Citlaly Nava, Carlos Villegas, Víctor Hugo Hernández Rodríguez, Aengus Anderson, Blanca Balderas and Víctor Hugo Medina, Marike Splint, the family of Jesus and Carmen Lopez, the Cocilovo family, and all the other incredible friends and creators who have anchored me through the years.

For welcoming me into their lives for so many years: Kirsten Boele and the Boele family.

For his care, his generosity of spirit, and for sharing his beautiful home—a place of immeasurable creative solace: Ron Simmons.

ACKNOWLEDGMENTS

For their kinship: Grace, Daven, Renn Tsalie, Beverly and Laf Young, Trevor Woolf, Susan Bratton, and the Carr family.

For my three fathers: Charles Simmons, Jack Utter, Al Carr.

For her partnership, her inspiration, and her luminous mind: Karima Walker.

WORKS CITED

BOOKS

Giorgio Agamben, *State of Exception* (translated by Kevin Attell)

Gloria E. Anzaldúa, "(Un)natural bridges, (Un)safe spaces," in *this bridge we call home: radical visions for transformation*, edited by Gloria E. Anzaldúa and AnaLouise Keating.

Charles Bowden and Molly Molloy (editors), *El Sicario: The Autobiography of a Mexican Assasin*

Judith Butler, *Precarious Life: The Powers of Mourning and Violence*

Jason de Leon, *Land of Open Graves: Living and Dying on the Migrant Trail*

David Dorado Romo, *Ringside Seat to a Revolution*

Jorge Durand (editor), *El norte es como el mar: entrevistas a trabajadores migrantes en Estados Unidos* (quotation translated by Francisco Cantú)

William H. Emory, *Report on the US and Mexican Boundary Survey*

Jack D. Forbes, *Columbus and Other Cannibals: The Wétiko Disease of Exploitation, Imperialism, and Terrorism*

Cristina Rivera Garza, *Dolerse* (English translation as "*To Be in Pain*" forthcoming from Jen Hofer)

Julian D. Hayden, *The Sierra Pinacate*

Dom Roger Hudleston (translator), *The Little Flowers of Saint Francis*

Derrick Jensen, *A Language Older Than Words*

Carl Jung, *The Undiscovered Self; Dreams;* and *Children's Dreams: Notes from the Seminar Given in 1936-1940*

Frank McLynn, *Villa and Zapata: A History of the Mexican Revolution*

Sandra Rodriguez Nieto, *The Story of Vicente, Who Murdered His Mother, His Father, and His Sister: Life and Death in Juárez* (translated by Daniela Maria Ugaz and John Washington)

Sergio González Rodríguez, *The Femicide Machine* (translated by Michael Parker-Stainback)

Susan Sontag, *Regarding the Pain of Others*

Timothy Snyder, *Bloodlands: Europe Between Hitler and Stalin*

Sara Uribe, *Antígona González* (translated by John Pluecker)

Sayak Valencia, *Gore Capitalism* (translated by John Pluecker)

Ed Vulliamy, *Amexica: War Along the Borderline*

David Wood, *What Have We Done: The Moral Injury of Our Longest Wars*

Jane Zavisca, "Metaphorical Imagery in News Reporting on Migrant Deaths," *Migrant Deaths in the Arizona Desert: La Vida No Vale Nada*, edited by Raquel Rubio-Goldsmith, Celestino Fernández, Jessie K. Finch, Araceli Masterson-Algar

ARTICLES, REPORTS, FILM, AND RADIO

BBC.com, "Are Murderers Born or Made?" (2015)

Tessie Borden, "INS: Border Policy Failed," *The Arizona Republic* (2000)

Damien Cave, "Wave of Violence Swallows More Women in Juárez," *The New York Times* (2012)

Manny Fernandez, "A Path to America, Marked by More and More Bodies," *The New York Times* (2017)

Daniel González and Rafael Carranza, "Is the Term "Tonc" an Acronym or Derogatory Term for Migrants?," *The Arizona Republic* (2018)

Christopher Hooks, "Q&A with Molly Molloy: The Story of the Juarez Femicides is a 'Myth,'" *The Texas Observer* (2014)

Joel Millman, "Immigrants Become Hostages as Gangs Prey on Mexicans," *The Wall Street Journal* (2009)

No More Deaths and La Coalición de Derechos Humanos, "The Disappeared Report" (2016)

Bob Ortega, "Border Patrol Failed to Count Hundreds of Migrant Deaths on US Soil," CNN.com (2018)

Pope Francis, "Visit to Lampedusa Homily," *The Holy See* (2013)

Radiolab, "Border Trilogy Part 2: Hold the Line," WNYC studios (2018)

WORKS CITED

Gianfranco Rosi (director), *El Sicario: Room 164* (2010)

Francis Stonor Saunders, "Where on Earth Are You?," *London Review of Books* (2016)

Julie Watson, "Mexico Morgues Crowded with Drug-War Dead," The Associated Press (2009)

FURTHER READING

Gloria Anzaldúa, *Borderlands/La Frontera: The New Mestiza*

Peg Bowden, *A Land of Hard Edges: Serving the Front Lines of the Border*

Bill Broyles, *Desert Duty: On the Line with the US Border Patrol*

Alfredo Corchado, *Midnight in Mexico: A Reporters Journey Through a Country's Descent into Darkness; Homelands: Four Friends, Two Countries, and the Fate of the Great Mexican-American Migration*

Guadalupe Correa-Cabrera, *Los Zetas Inc.: Criminal Corporations, Energy, and Civil War in Mexico*

CrimethInc ex-Worker's Collective, *No Wall They Can Build: A Guide to Borders & Migration Across North America*

Melissa del Bosque, *Bloodlines: How the FBI took on Mexico's Most Violent Drugs Cartel*

Kathryn Ferguson, Norma A. Price, and Ted Parks (editors), *Crossing with the Virgin: Stories from the Migrant Trail*

John Gibler, *To Die in Mexico: Disptaches from Inside the Drug War*

Reyna Grande, *The Distance Between Us* and *A Dream Called Home*

Stephanie Elizondo Griest, *All the Agents and Saints: Dispatches from the US Borderlands*

Roger D. Hodge, *Texas Blood: Seven Generations Among the Outlaws, Ranchers, Indians, Missionaries, Soldiers, and Smugglers of the Borderlands*

Karl Jacoby, *Shadows at Dawn: An Apache Massacre and the Violence of History*

Mark Klett, *The Devil's Highway* (photographs)

Valeria Luiselli, *Tell Me How It Ends: An Essay in 40 Questions*

Kelly Lytle Hernández, *Migra!: A History of the US Border Patrol*

Lauren Markham, *The Faraway Brothers: Two Young Migrants and the Making of an American Life*

Óscar Martínez, *The Beast: Riding the Rails and Dodging Narcos on the Migrant Trail*

Rubén Martínez, *Crossing Over: A Mexican Family on the Migrant Trail* and *Desert America: A Journey Through Our Most Divided Landscape*

Todd Miller, *Border Patrol Nation: Dispatches from the Front Lines of Homeland Security* and *Storming the Wall: Climate Change, Migration, and Homeland Security*

Richard Misrach and Guillermo Galindo, *Border Cantos*

José Ángel N., *Illegal: Reflections of an Undocumented Immigrant*

Sonia Nazario, *Enrique's Journey: The Story of a Boy's Dangerous Odyssey to Reunite with His Mother*

José Olivarez, *Citizen Illegal: Poems*

Dawn Paley, *Drug War Capitalism*

Ronald Rael, *Borderwall as Architecture: A Manifesto for the US-Mexico Boundary*

Jorge Ramos, *Stranger: The Challenge of a Latino Immigrant in the Trump Era*

Margaret Regan, *The Death of Josseline: Immigration Stories from the Arizona-Mexico Borderlands* and *Detained and Deported: Stories of Immigrant Families Under Fire*

Natalie Scenters-Zapico, *The Verging Cities: Poems*

Rachel St. John, *Line in the Sand: A History of the Western US-Mexico Border*

David Taylor, *Working the Line* (photographs) and *Monuments* (photographs)

Luis Alberto Urrea, *The Devil's Highway*

Jose Antonio Vargas, *Dear America: Notes of an Undocumented Citizen*

Vanessa Angélica Villarreal, *Beast Meridian: Poems*

Javier Zamora, *Unaccompanied: Poems*

Ofelia Zepeda, *Ocean Power: Poems; Where Clouds Are Formed: Poems*

The organizations listed below have robust advocacy programs in the borderlands and are set up to receive tax-deductible donations. Many of them also offer volunteer opportunities. For more information about advocacy organizations, visit https://www.penguinrandomhouse.com/books/555764 /the-line-becomes-a-river-by-francisco-cantu/9780735217713/readers -guide/.

The Colibri Center for Human Rights (http://www.colibricenter.org) is dedicated to the idea that no human being should lose their life crossing a border and no family should experience the pain of searching for them. By partnering with families and forensic scientists, they help to identify people who have lost their lives in the desert.

Border Angels (https://www.borderangels.org) is an all-volunteer nonprofit that seeks to promote human rights, social justice, and humane immigration reform. Volunteer opportunities include outreach to day laborers and monitoring water stations along the California border.

No More Deaths (http://forms.nomoredeaths.org/about-no-more-deaths/) is a humanitarian organization located in southern Arizona that works to end migrant death and suffering in the U.S.-Mexico borderlands. They offer a variety of field-based volunteer programs in the desert of Arizona.

The Texas Civil Rights Project (https://texascivilrightsproject.org) assists families at the border to get translation services and legal advice; more broadly, the organization works to reform the criminal justice system, advance racial and economic justice, and protect voting rights.

Mariposas Sin Fronteras (https://mariposassinfronteras.org) seeks to end violence and abuse against LGBTQ people held in prison and immigration detention by supporting detainees through visits, letters, bond support, advocacy, and housing upon freedom from detention.

The National Network for Immigrant and Refugee Rights (http://www .nnirr.org) works to defend and expand the rights of all refugees and immigrants, regardless of immigration status.

The Kino Border Initiative (https://www.kinoborderinitiative.org/) works to promote immigration and border policies that affirm human dignity. The organization offers educational opportunities, immersion experiences, and volunteer programs at their aid center and soup kitchen for deported migrants.

The Florence Immigrant and Refugee Rights Project (https://firrp.org) works to provide free legal and social services to detained immigrant men, women, and unaccompanied minors under threat of deportation in Arizona.

The Refugee and Immigrant Center for Education and Legal Services (https://www.raicestexas.org) the largest immigration legal services provider in Texas, offering free and low-cost legal services to families, refugees, and immigrant children in Central and South Texas.

The Cristo Rey Border Immersion Program (http://iglesiacristorey.wix site.com/borderimmersion) invites participants to learn more about issues that affect those living in the borderlands. This program allows participants to participate in fellowship at the El Paso-Ciudad Juarez fence, tour rural settlements in El Paso, assist with after school programs, and more.

BorderLinks (https://www.borderlinks.org/) facilitates educational cross-border immersion trips to the Arizona-Sonora border region to raise awareness about the impact of border and immigration policies through field-based experiential learning that emphasizes migrant voices and social change.